AUSTRALIA AND THE INDIAN OCEAN

Centre for Indian Ocean Regional Studies
Curtin University of Technology
GPO Box U1987, Perth, Western Australia 6001

Director: Dr Kenneth McPherson

Studies in Indian Ocean Maritime Affairs

1. **Australia and the Indian Ocean: Strategic Dimensions of Increasing Naval Involvement.** Edited by Robert H. Bruce, 1988.

AUSTRALIA AND THE INDIAN OCEAN

STRATEGIC DIMENSIONS OF INCREASING NAVAL INVOLVEMENT

Edited by Robert H. Bruce

Studies in Indian Ocean Maritime Affairs, Number 1

Centre for Indian Ocean Regional Studies
Curtin University of Technology
Perth, Australia

ISBN 0 909848 91 2

CONTENTS

Contributors i

Foreword iii
Professor Peter Reeves

Preface v
Robert H. Bruce

Introduction: Naval Policy, Strategic Environment, and Critical Questions 1
Robert H. Bruce

Part 1: Policy of Increasing Australian Naval Involvement in the Indian Ocean

1. The Two Ocean Navy 9
   Kim C. Beazley

Part 2: Strategic Environment and Policy Responses: Assessments

2. From Dante to Shannon: The Indian Ocean in Australia's Strategic Environment 21
   Michael McKinley
   Comments: Hugh Collins
   Peter Reeves
3. The 1987 Defence White Paper: A Maritime Perspective 47
   A.J. Robertson
   Comments: Frank Broeze
   P.G.N. Kennedy
   Robert H. Bruce
4. Strategic Developments in the Indian and South Pacific Ocean Regions 79
   K. Subrahmanyam
   Comments: Mohammed Ayoob

Part 3: Focus on the Persian Gulf: The United States and Australia

5. US Military Build-up in the Persian Gulf: Limitations and Risks 103
   Rasul B. Rais
   Comments: Mohammed Ayoob
6. Australia and the Persian Gulf Conflict: The Public Perception of the War 122
   Claude G.P. Rakisits

CONTRIBUTORS

Mohammed Ayoob is a member of the Institute of Southeast Asian Studies, Singapore.

Kim C. Beazley is Minister of Defence, Australia.

Frank Broeze is Associate Professor of History, University of Western Australia, Perth, Australia.

Robert H. Bruce is Senior Lecturer in Politics, Curtin University of Technology, Perth, Australia.

Hugh Collins is Professor of Government and Politics, Murdoch University, Perth, Australia.

P.G.N. Kennedy is a Rear Admiral (Rtd) in the Royal Australian Navy.

Michael McKinley was until May 1988 Lecturer in International Relations and Strategic Studies, University of Western Australia, and is now Lecturer in International Relations, Australian National University, Canberra, Australia.

Rasul A. Rais is Associate Professor in International Relations, Quaid-i-Azam University, Pakistan.

Claude G.P. Rakisits is a member of the Foreign Affairs Group, Legislative Reference Service, Department of the Parliamentary Library, Parliament House, Canberra, Australia.

Peter Reeves is Professor and Deputy Vice-Chancellor, Division of Arts, Education and Social Sciences, Curtin University of Technology, Perth, Australia.

A.J. Robertson is a Rear Admiral (Rtd), Royal Australian Navy, and Senior Vice President of the Navy League of Australia.

K. Subrahmanyam is Jawaharal Nehru Memorial Visiting Professor at St John's College, Cambridge University in the United Kingdom and former Director of the Institute for Defence Studies and Analyses, New Delhi, India.

FOREWORD

This is the first volume in an Indian Ocean Maritime Affairs series to be published by the Centre for Indian Ocean Regional Studies at Curtin University of Technology. It derives from a seminar held by the Centre in Fremantle in March 1988. The Centre was established in 1986 to promote understanding of the Indian Ocean region in Australia generally and in Western Australia in particular. Curtin has always taken its international links and obligations very seriously and the Centre for Indian Ocean Regional Studies is the most recent manifestation of that concern.

The Centre's programmes are posited on a belief in the importance of the Indian Ocean Region—politically, economically and culturally—and especially a belief in the importance of the region for Australia's future. The Centre seeks to promote understanding of the region through seminars and conferences, a range of publications, and organised research and teaching programmes. Its **Indian Ocean Newsletter** was started in 1980 by the Centre's Director, Dr Kenneth McPherson, who continues to edit the successor to the **Newsletter, The Indian Ocean Review.** This present volume will be followed this year by an Indian Ocean Atlas, a volume of essays on the development of the Indian Navy, a major bibliography on modern Indian Ocean ports and research monographs derived from the Centre's research programme (supported by funding from the Australian Research Grants Committee for the past three years) on trading and shipping networks of the region, especially in the period from 1870 to 1940.

The Centre is interested in the region as a whole. There is little doubt that as a region the Indian Ocean today is not as well-integrated as it was in the period before the European entry at the end of the 15th century. In that period before the European encroachment, it was possible to see the area dominated by the monsoons as a clear regional entity. Those monsoon winds are created by the physical configuration of the Ocean: it is the only one of the great oceans which is blocked to the north by a major land mass and which, as a result, has that system of seasonal winds. That wind system made possible, in turn, the great sailing traffic of the region on the basis of which grew a trading network linking the highly developed littoral civilizations that flourished over the two millennia after 500BC.

From the development of the trading network came cultural interaction which further reinforced the linkages through the region. One can look at the spread of Islam from the mid-7th century onwards—or of Hinduism and Buddhism in even earlier periods—for examples of cultural diffusion through the sailing-trading network which had been built up. Some of these underlying elements of regional identity are still important today, even though the development of nation states following the experience of European colonial rule has altered very dramatically the structure and the ethos of the region. Those of us involved in the Centre believe, therefore, that we need to be able to appreciate those underlying elements of regional identity if we are to understand the region today.

Dr McPherson and I welcome contact with all those who share the Centre's interest in the region and who would like to participate in future activities, use the Centre's expertise, obtain the Centre's publications and/or share experience in common fields of endeavour.

Professor Peter Reeves
Chairman, Management Committee, CIORS
and
Deputy Vice-Chancellor,
Arts, Education and Social Sciences,
Curtin University of Technology

PREFACE

This volume originated in a seminar, "Australia and the Indian Ocean: The Strategic Dimensions of Australia's Increasing Naval Involvement in the Indian Ocean," organized by the Centre for Indian Ocean Regional Studies (CIORS), Curtin University of Technology, Perth, Western Australia. The seminar was held 28-30 March 1988 in Fremantle, Western Australia.

Professor Peter Reeves, Chairman of the Management Committee of CIORS, and Dr Kenneth McPherson, Director of CIORS, were the driving forces behind the seminar. Kenneth McPherson took an idea for the seminar and made it into a reality with exceptional organizational skills and hard work. This volume of papers and comments from that seminar exists because of his efforts.

Both the Rural & Industries Bank of Western Australia and Australian Marine Systems Pty Ltd supported the seminar, and the final volume took physical shape with the active support of Dr Joan Wardrop, Beverley and Carole Bardwell-Dix, Joan Kimber, Beverley Priest and Kylie Byfield.

INTRODUCTION

Naval Policy, Strategic Environment, and Critical Questions

Robert H. Bruce

The topic of this volume of papers and comments from the seminar on "Australia and Indian Ocean" is the strategic environment within which Australia operates on the Indian Ocean, and the policy of increasing Australian naval involvement there in response to that strategic environment. The unity of this volume around that topic finds expression in two ways.

The first is the more obvious unity of the formal structure of the volume as laid out in the table of contents. There are parts and chapters, followed by comments on chapters, that elaborate on the strategic environment and/or increasing Australian naval involvement in the Indian Ocean. In the first part and Chapter 1, Kim Beazley, Australian Minister of Defence and architect of the policy of increasing naval involvement there, describes and explains the policy. In the second part, three chapters and subsequent comments discuss and evaluate aspects of the policy and/or the strategic context of that policy. In Chapter 2, Michael McKinley puts that policy into historical and strategic perspective. Hugh Collins and Peter Reeves comment on points made in Chapters 1 and 2. In Chapter 3, A.J. Robertson evaluates the maritime aspects of that policy. Frank Broeze, P.G.N. Kennedy and Robert Bruce comment on that and earlier chapters. In Chapter 4, K. Subrahmanyam examines the larger and changing geopolitical context within which Australia's increasing naval involvement on the Indian Ocean occurs. Mohammed Ayoob comments on that chapter. Part three focuses on the Persian Gulf, the one area of the Indian Ocean where active warfare occurs, which is important to Australia because of oil imports and trade, and where Australia's policy is controversial. In Chapter 5, Rasul Rais examines the complexities of the war and the nature of United States involvement there. Mohammed Ayoob comments. This chapter and comments provide the background for Claude Rakisits' examination of the relationship between Australia and that conflict in the Persian Gulf in Chapter 6. These relations of chapters and comments to the central topic of this volume are more obvious than the second way the unity finds expression.

The second way the unity is expressed is less obvious, more elusive, but nevertheless equally, if not more, important than the first way. It is the unity of a dialogue on the policy of increasing Australian naval involvement in the Indian Ocean. It places the policy as enunciated by Kim Beazley in Chapter 1—and by extension of the Defence White Paper* on which it is based—at the centre of attention. The policy is an answer to a question: What is the best way to ensure Australia's security? Other contributors to this volume, by the points they make in their chapters or comments, raise important questions about that policy as the answer to the question of how to best ensure Australia's security.

These questions are important. Good questions animate inquiry, guide the search for answers, and precede understanding. Good questions need to be asked about Australia's policy of increasing naval involvement in the Indian Ocean. The diversity of contributors to this volume and the different aspects of the policy they examine stimulate many questions about the policy as a response to the strategic environment.

By organizing these questions into three categories some order can be brought to the large number and complexity of the questions. There are questions about the premises upon which the policy is based, questions about policy conclusions drawn from the premises, and questions about the completeness of the analysis involved in formulating the policy. This second way the unity of this volume is expressed does not conform to the formal organization of the book, except insofar as the policy described in

---

* Numerous references are made to this important document in the chapters and comments in this volume. Departments of Defence, **The Defence of Australia 1987** (Canberra: Australian Government Publishing Service, 1987).

Chapter 1 is followed by the questions raised by other contributors in subsequent chapters and comments. The three categories of questions cut across these later chapters and comments; they help to organize and integrate points made by contributors in chapters and comments into a dialogue with Kim Beazley on the policy of increasing naval involvement in the Indian Ocean spelled out in Chapter 1. Each of the categories and examples of questions raised are briefly examined below.

The first category raises questions about the adequacy of the premises upon which the policy is based. The premises consist of facts, interpretations of those facts, and assumptions about such things as the threats to Australia now and in the future, Australia's vulnerability, developments in military technology, continuity of domestic political support and funding, and so on. Not all of the premises are stated explicitly; some are implicit. Questions raised in the first category are about the adequacy of these premises upon which the policy is based; a change in premise would imply a change in the appropriate policy conclusion. A brief discussion of several examples will indicate the nature of the questions raised in the first category. The policy is based upon a conception of Australia's area of strategic interest. Yet Robertson (in Chapter 3) and Broeze (in comments after Chapter 3), for example, raise questions about the adequacy of the geographic scope of the area of strategic interest. Both suggest that it is too limited; an important premise upon which the policy is based is wrong, they contend. The policy pays little attention to China and Japan. Yet, Subrahmanyam (in Chapter 4) and Ayoob (in comments after Chapter 4) discuss the need to understand the linkages between the northwest Pacific Ocean and the Indian Ocean and the importance of both countries for Australian defence in a changing strategic environment. Both suggest that this omission needs to be rectified; important factors in Australia's strategic environment are missing from the premises upon which the policy conclusions are based. Other examples of questions raised in this first category included the adequacy of implicit assumptions about changing military technologies (Subrahamanyam in Chapter 4), about the security relationship with the United States that underpins the policy (Bruce in comments after Chapter 3), and about the threat to Australia in the future posed by the Indian navy (Robertson in Chapter 3).

The second category raises questions about the validity of the policy conclusions drawn from the premises. The policy embraces the use of conventionally powered submarines, for example. Yet Robertson (in Chapter 3) raises questions about it and suggests that nuclear powered submarines are better. This reflects, in part, questions he raised about the adequacy of the geographic scope of Australia's area of strategic interest. An expanded area of strategic interest would alter the policy conclusions; nuclear submarines become more appropriate if there is a need for Australian submarines to operate in a larger area. But it also reflects a different conclusion drawn from the premises. Michael McKinley notes in Chapter 2 that "previous policies remained so bereft of substance that they could not be seen as other than an illogical inference from the objective circumstances as they were understood." Now, he argues, better policy conclusions are beginning to be drawn. Yet, logical errors in inferring policy conclusions from the premises upon which they are based remain according to questions raised in the second category.

The third category of questions raised about the policy to increase Australian naval involvement in the Indian Ocean is of a different nature than the other two categories. Here questions are raised about the completeness of the analysis; the questions point to the need for the analysis that produced the premises and policy conclusions to cast its net wider in order to be satisfactory. In this category, for example, are questions about whether the policy and the Defence White Paper actually are a blueprint for solving the problem of ensuring Australia's security that the Beazley chapter and White Paper set out to solve. On a smaller scale, McKinley in (Chapter 2) raises questions about the gap in analysis involving Christmas Island and the Cocos Islands. On a much grander scale, questions are raised about whether the policy has been placed into the larger context of Australia's overall strategy of achieving its objectives in dealing with other states. What may be missing in the analysis is a careful consideration of what Australia wants to achieve, the interests it needs to protect in order to achieve those goals, the selection of the appropriate mix of political, economic, and military instruments to achieve those goals. McKinley (in Chapter 2) notes that military policy seems to dominate foreign policy. Collins (in comments after Chapter 2) notes the problem of coordinating foreign and military policies. Bruce (in comments after Chapter 3) claims inadequate consideration is given to the implications of the policy for relations with other states. Broeze (in comments after Chapter 3) wonders about the configuration of Australian naval forces for achievement of political objectives.

The dialogue between the Minister of Defence, who is the architect of the policy, on the one hand, and other contributors, by questions raised in the three categories about the policy, is the second way the volume is unified around the topic. Overall, this volume contributes to an increased understanding of Australia's strategic environment, the policy of increasing naval involvement in the Indian Ocean, and critical questions about that policy's appropriateness as a response to that strategic environment.

PART 1

Policy of Increasing Naval Involvement in the Indian Ocean

CHAPTER 1

The Two Ocean Navy

Kim C. Beazley

It is an interesting reflection on the strategic perceptions of Australians that the decision to base our Navy on the Indian Ocean as well as the Pacific has come so late in our history.

The Indian Ocean has been a strategic conundrum for Australians ever since they first started thinking about their strategic circumstances in a coherent way last century. So it is not surprising that people are curious about the reasoning behind decisions by this government to expand our defence presence on our Indian Ocean coast.

My aim here is to explain how these decisions fit into the government's broader strategic policies, and in particular what they mean for our view of the Indian Ocean.

The fact that such an explanation is required at all shows how different our strategic perceptions of the Indian Ocean are from those of the Pacific.

Viewed from Australia, the strategic geography of the South Pacific is fairly clear. A chain of islands stretches across the approaches to Australia, relatively close to our shores. The friendly control of those islands has always been an important strategic interest to Australia, and throughout the nineteenth century we watched with interest as their control was contested between a number of colonial powers—Germany, US, Britain, France, Japan and even, by repute, Russia.

An important element of the strategic environment of the Pacific at that time was that British naval power was not predominant in the Pacific for most of the 19th century.

By contrast Australia's strategic interests in the Indian Ocean have been seen much less clearly.

Partly this was because the Indian Ocean has been less threatening to Australia's peace of mind than has the Pacific. Unlike the Pacific, the Indian Ocean has been, for most of Australia's history, very much a British lake. British control of the Cape, Aden, India and Singapore, and much of the Littoral, gave the British a very strong naval position there.

Secondly, the Indian Ocean is, when viewed from Australia, a lot emptier than the South Pacific. No island chains straddle our near approaches in the Indian Ocean the way the islands of the Pacific do. The islands of the Indian Ocean do not look to Australia for trade, aid, education, and security, the way the islands of the Pacific do.

And thirdly, as all West Australians know, the Indian Ocean is a long way from the homes of most Australians.

Nonetheless, Australians from all over the continent have long felt vaguely uneasy about our long, open western coastline. Plans were made as long ago as 1911 to build a major naval base in WA, but little was actually done. Then in the early 1970's a major naval base was built at Garden Island, but no major fleet units were deployed here.

Now the government has decided to move about half the fleet to WA, and substantially expand both our surface and submarine capabilities, giving Australia for the first time a genuine two-ocean navy. In view of the uncertainties and ambiguities of Australia's perceptions of our Indian Ocean strategic requirements, the question arises why the decision has been made now to move half the fleet to the west.

The history of Australia's defence policy has tended to be a history of ad hoc responses to external events. So the natural conclusion drawn by observers of our military affairs is that the two ocean navy is most probably a response to specific external developments.

This is not the case. The Indian Ocean has seen important strategic changes in recent years, and developments there are carefully studied.

Over the last 20 years or so we have witnessed the emergence of a wider range of influences and developments in the Indian Ocean region. Notable among these have been the uneven and frequently turbulent process of decolonization, the withdrawal of

British forces east of Suez which was announced in 1967, the regular deployment of small Soviet naval forces since 1968, including the use of support facilities at Yemen and Sokotra; the expansion of the US naval presence, including the development of Diego Garcia as a major base and an increase in regional conflicts, including the Indo-Pakistani wars, Afghanistan and the Gulf War. However, the presence of external naval forces fluctuates greatly. The Indian Ocean is low on the list of superpower priorities. The participation of the navies of the superpowers and other external powers in ensuring freedom of navigation in the Gulf very much conceals what was a declining interest. From an average of around 50 visits a year in the early 1980s, visits to Western Australia by US warships declined to 35 in 1987. With any diminishing threat to Gulf shipping and expenditure cuts in the superpowers this trend would likely reassert itself.

However, several Indian Ocean littoral states have developed their maritime power from the very low base of naval infrastructure developed by the colonial powers. For example, Pakistan and South Africa have enhanced their naval strength over the last four decades. Notably, both countries have opted not to expand significantly their destroyer, frigate or afloat support capabilities. However, they have diversified their forces by adding modern small submarines and missile attack craft suitable primarily for sea denial operations in coastal waters. With the notable exception of India, regional maritime forces still lack the balanced force structure and sufficiently developed infrastructure which would allow the projection of sustained military power outside contiguous waters. There is little prospect of most Indian Ocean nations being able to threaten effectively nations at some distance, or to interdict internationally-important mid-ocean shipping lanes. They remain concerned primarily with operations in their coastal waters which are very remote from Australia. This will be likely to remain true for at least the foreseeable future.

Maritime conflict in the Indian Ocean region is and will continue to be more likely between adjacent hostile states that can use their limited maritime capability in areas close to their bases and infrastructure. The situation in the Persian Gulf is a good example.

The Indian posture is nevertheless intriguing. At the outset I should say India has never, and does not threaten Australia. It is well distant from us but relations since Indian independence have varied from the correct to the very friendly. They have never been hostile. India's overall strategic context justifies a substantial navy. India has an extensive coastline. It has strategic concerns well out into the north-west Indian Ocean and the Bay of Bengal. Given India's fierce attitude to its independence of action in world affairs it would wish to be invulnerable to superpower pressure. Superpower operations in India's direct area of interest have been extensive.

Having said all that, and again reiterating our confidence in good relations with India, noting too the fact India is 5,500km from Australia, any development of a force projection capability in our general region must interest us. We have the answers in our own inventory with air and subsurface maritime strike so we ought not to be overly concerned. We also have small projection capabilities ourselves. In India's case the possession of a substantial number of carriers, the possibility of balanced carrier battle groups and submarines, poses possibilities for extensively increased Indian influence at the major eastern Indian Ocean choke points. We are active in defence undertakings in this area and will watch diplomatic developments carefully.

But these developments do not directly influence our decisions about the structure and deployment of our armed forces. This government's defence policy derives from a systematic analysis of our fundamental strategic priority, which is the defence of Australian territory. That analysis necessarily focuses on the most fundamental and permanent features of our strategic situation.

Our decision to base half the fleet in Western Australia derives directly from that analysis. While Australia does not face a direct threat, it faces a complex strategic environment in which conflicts could arise which did not automatically involve the interests of our major allies. This requires a defence policy which recognises the importance of both:

- maintaining and developing capabilities for the independent defence of Australia and its interests; and
- promoting strategic stability and security in our region.

Such a policy requires that we develop the capability to operate effectively throughout the maritime approaches on both sides of the continent and to be in a position to make a meaningful contribution to regional security interests. The development of a genuine "two ocean" navy through the establishment of a major naval base on the west coast and a significant enhancement of our surface and submarine forces is fundamental to realising these objectives.

First, the development of a major fleet base at Cockburn Sound. I'm sure you will be aware of this decision, made in February 1987 following consideration of the fleet base relocation study, which addressed the options for relocating major fleet elements from Sydney.

The development of HMAS Stirling as a major naval support facility dates from 1972, when the project was announced. The base opened in 1978 with facilities to support four escort vessels and three submarines. Before 1984, however, the largest combat vessel based at Stirling was a patrol boat, although the facility was used as a staging base for fleet deployments and naval exercises in the west and north west.

Since then, use of the base has progressively expanded. The destroyer escort HMAS Stuart was home-ported to Stirling in 1984 and HMAS Swan followed in 1985. In December 1985 it was announced that Stirling would be developed as a major submarine base, HMAS Oxley was home-ported in September 1987. Two Fremantle class patrol boats, the survey ship HMAS Moresby and a reserve attack class patrol boat are also currently based in Western Australia.

This government has given a high priority to the expansion of Stirling's role in recognition of the importance of the base in promoting both our self-reliant strategic posture and our ability to pursue our regional and alliance objectives by enhancing the fleet's access to areas of direct military interest.

The precise composition, and balance of capabilities to be based at Stirling is currently being examined within the Defence Department. I expect to be advised of options concerning the priority and timing of deployment of various fleet elements following departmental consideration. Some major priorities have already been announced. For example, the government has already decided that HMAS Stirling will be the major RAN submarine base. Eventually four of our six new submarines will be based permanently in the west. As Australia's premier submarine base, Stirling will be restoring the situation that existed in World War II when there were extensive submarine operations from Fremantle.

The relocation of about half the fleet will be an extremely complex exercise. At this stage it is estimated the whole programme will take about 10 years.

The decision to develop HMAS Stirling as a major naval base should be seen in terms of its contribution to our major defence policy objectives. In particular the expansion of operations from Stirling will enhance markedly the RAN's ability to sustain operations in our strategically important northern and north western maritime approaches. The flexibility and effectiveness of RAN operations in these areas will be increased. The navy will also be more readily able to exercise and develop expertise in our northern waters where it would be most likely to operate should a defence contingency arise.

Vessels operating in the north and north west from Stirling will gain a substantial increase in effective time compared with fleet units from east coast bases. The shorter transit times from Stirling will mean that surface units will gain about 13% effective operating time and submarines—for which transit time is more critical—about 31%.

The development of Stirling will also enable the Navy, which traditionally plays a very important role in the promotion of our regional defence activities, presence and influence, to support these objectives more effectively. Stirling is much closer to our neighbours in South East Asia, than our east coast bases. In fact, the transit time from Stirling to Jakarta and Singapore is only about half that from Sydney. Using Stirling, naval deployments to Singapore, for example, would save almost six days steaming time.

This development has been at the heart of an initiative I recently announced to rotate a ship/submarine permanently through Malaysia and Singapore. Western basing makes this initiative considerably cheaper.

An area of high priority is the development of major facilities associated with the expansion of Stirling. The government is determined that the two ocean navy does not become a hollow tag, devoid of substance. We are not in the game of moving half the fleet to the west without planning for the means to make the initiative worthwhile. I make no apologies for the fact that the creation of a genuine two ocean capability will be expensive. The important thing is to view the costs in relation to the benefits, which are substantial.

Works associated with the development are currently estimated to cost some $300 million over 10 years and will involve the relocation of some 3000 navy personnel and their dependents, raising the total number of service personnel and their dependents located in the west to some 5500 by the year 2000.

Major facilities development will include a submarine escape training facility, which is nearing completion, the new RAN submarine school, and a civil-operated ship-lift facility at Jervoise Bay is expected to be operational by the end of this year and will be capable of meeting the RAN's docking and refitting requirements.

The development of HMAS Stirling will have major local impact. Consideration by the West Australian Department of Industrial Development suggests that the overall impact of the two ocean basing policy could result in an increase in local demand for consumer goods in the order of $25m annually and create in excess of 450 permanent new jobs and up to 1000 temporary ones in the construction stages. An additional 520 houses costing some $41.5m will be progressively built throughout the project.

The decision to base about half the fleet at Stirling is only part of the creation of a two ocean navy. The importance of facilities developments at HMAS Stirling should be viewed in conjunction with the government's new approach to naval force development which will contribute significantly to the RAN's ability to operate effectively on a two ocean basis.

The defence programme outlined in the White Paper includes the most radical revision of the Navy's surface combatant force structure in the RAN's history. For the last 40 years the RAN surface combatant force typically comprised about 12 major ships. These were configured to escort aircraft carriers in task forces, a role appropriate to the circumstances and requirements of the "forward defence" strategy.

The new surface fleet will contain three broad levels of capability. The highest level will be represented by the larger ships—destroyers and frigates; the second level by the new

ANZAC ships and the third level by the patrol boat force. The three tier concept allows us to have a navy more relevant to our strategic circumstances. It will enable more ships than before to be available for operations in support of both our own national security requirements and the promotion of our regional presence and influence.

The 1987 White Paper outlined the government's plan to increased the number of major surface combatants in the RAN—those in the first and second tiers—to 16 or 17. This programme will provide Australia with more major vessels designed to operate in the types of defence contingencies that could arise in the shorter term and will assure effective maintenance of those complex skills relevant to more substantial conflict. The additional numbers will enable the RAN to operate effectively from bases on both the east and west coasts on a routine basis.

The light patrol frigate project, or ANZAC ship project as it is now known, is a major collaborative Australian/New Zealand venture to enhance our respective maritime warfare capabilities. The project currently provides for construction of eight ships for the RAN and up to four ships for the Royal New Zealand Navy. A ceiling cost of $3.5 billion has been set for all activities associated with the procurement, outfitting and support of the eight ships for Australia. The selection of two designers was announced in January and we envisage letting the construction contract in about mid 1989 with first delivery in the early to mid 1990s.

The ANZAC ship project is a fundamental component of the government's initiatives both to increase the RAN's major surface combatant force and create a two ocean navy. Not only will the Navy have more major ships than before, but the force will be more balanced, more flexible and more appropriate to our unique strategic circumstances. The capability concept adopted for the ANZAC frigates embodies the same principles that guide the development of the Defence Force generally.

Initially the new ships will be equipped with an array of state-of-the-art weapons and sensors appropriate to those tasks that are important in the types of more limited conflict that are credible in the shorter term. However, they will retain sufficient space and weight to accommodate substantial capability enhancement to enable them to operate effectively in more serious conflicts should this ever become necessary.

Special consideration has been given to ensure that the ANZAC ships have exceptional range and endurance. This will enable them to operate effectively and flexibly throughout our area of direct military interest. About half of the new ships will be based at Stirling progressively as they enter service through the 1990s and beyond.

I have already mentioned the importance of basing four of our new submarines at Stirling for the development of a two ocean navy. The upgrading of our submarine fleet runs in tandem with the upgrading of the capability of our surface fleet.

The six new Kockums type 471 submarines to be built in Australia to replace the Oberons will be the largest, longest ranging and most lethal conventional submarines in the western world when they enter service in the 1990s. The new submarines will increase our maritime surveillance capabilities as well as providing a formidable strike capability.

The first submarine, fully outfitted, tested and trialled, will be delivered in January 1995. Subsequent submarines will be delivered at roughly 12-month intervals.

These many elements of our present defence policy cannot be seen as separate and distinct from each other. I have tried to show in outline how the two ocean navy is part of a larger design. That larger design is the result of the most rigorous defence analysis in Australia's history and I refer to 15 or more years of endeavour, not only to that of the last five years. The defence policy interlocks a strategic imperative—self reliance, a strategy-defence in depth, our regional relationships and our alliance relationships into one cohesive structure in which the key elements are mutually reinforcing. This cohesion is largely the achievement of the present government.

Within that policy, initiatives such as the development of HMAS Stirling, the increase in major surface combatant numbers, the enhancement of our submarine force, the development of a capable mine countermeasures force and the improvement of afloat logistic support capabilities cannot be viewed as isolated or ad hoc developments.

Taken together they will ensure that the Navy maintains a balance of skills and capabilities appropriate to our strategic circumstances as we approach the next century.

The development of a two ocean navy is central to this process. It is fundamental to improving defence self-reliance, our contribution to regional stability and our support for allies which underpin our defence policy.

PART 2

Strategic Environment and Policy Responses: Assessments

CHAPTER 2

From Dante to Shannon: The Indian Ocean in Australia's Strategic Environment

Michael McKinley

Should an intelligent observer from another planet, or even another country, be sequestered in one of the many luxurious hotels that now adorn Sydney or Melbourne and presented with the relevant literature and documentation, he or she could be forgiven for concluding that the Indian Ocean was Australia's foreign and defence policy enigma. This person would no doubt be puzzled as to why, when this country's north-west is just about its most resource-rich area, so few defence assets are devoted to its protection; why, when its Indian Ocean coast is its most vulnerable littoral, it took until the 1980s to permanently establish a surface combatant presence from the Royal Australian Navy on it; and why, when any significant military threat to Australia could only be projected from, or through the extensive archipelago to the north, the role which Western Australia should perform in the defence of the continent has been substantially neglected until relatively recent times. The conclusion such an observer might arrive at would no doubt embody the notion that, in the higher realms of Australian security policy making, and in relation to the west and northwest of the country's strategic environment, logic was a dispensable, and cognitive disonance an acceptable, virtue. Australia's strategic policy, it seems, was inspired not by Mahan, as might have been expected, but by Dante's injunction "non regioniam di lor, ma guarda e passa" ("speak not of them, but look and pass them by"). Such a view would be warranted, of course, if the Indian Ocean was without menace or if the Ocean itself comprised an insignificant sea line of communication (SLOC), or if Western, and North Western Australia's strategic assets were so without value that their loss could be accepted with equanimity. In fact, though, none of these is true.

To understand this claim it is important, first, to grasp the essentially complex nature of the Indian Ocean basin. Within the 44 independent nations washed by the Indian Ocean are found Arab, African, European, Indian and Malay peoples practising the faiths of Buddhism, Christianity, Hinduism and Islam. Taken together they constitute nearly one-third of the world's population, but this statistic by itself obscures the range of contrast—from India with more than 700 million down to Comoros with fewer than 500,000. More importantly, the region is host to a representative sample of the major ills which beset political society, domestic and international, in the closing years of the twentieth century. It is a pathology whose constituent parts include political and social deprivation, economic under-development, colonial and post-colonial exploitation, racism, sectarianism and dynastic differences. The politics of much of the region tend, therefore, to be characterised by the relative fragility and vulnerability of democratic institutions, where they exist, but transcending this, almost permanent conflict, particularly in the so-called "arc of instability" which stretches from the Horn of Africa round to the Indian subcontinent, including the hinterland of the littoral states. Furthermore in the eastern recesses of the eastern Indian Ocean lies what is arguably Australia's greatest external security preoccupation in the form of border tensions between Indonesia and Papua New Guinea.

One of the serious consequences of this condition has been the frantic race for arms within the region to the point where it now includes one of the world's largest military powers—India—and at least four of the world's actual and potential nuclear proliferators—India, Israel, Pakistani and South Africa. By virtue of this fact alone, the region has attracted various manifestations of interest by external powers, from attention, to presence, to outright interference. Overall, so riven with externally induced (and internally generated) tension and conflict is it that the Indian Ocean basin does not so much describe a region as it does the geographic setting for fissiparous forces which result in a collection of sub-regions.

It would, however, be a cruelly distorted analysis which claimed that the regional peoples were *entirely* responsible for their own predicament. Indeed, it is, perhaps, their misfortune to inhabit lands which, irrespective of their intrinsic status, were bound to achieve significance in the context of the global strategic rivalries between the superpowers and their respective alliance and trading systems. Because it lies at the intersection of three continents; because its under-water topography is ideally suited for locating strategic nuclear systems; because the bulk of the non-communist world's proven oil resources are located near it (including Japan's total supplies); because its surface waterways carry the strategic raw materials and trade products of much of the industrialised world; and because its seabed is a repository for essential high-grade minerals, the Indian Ocean is accorded fundamental strategic importance.[1] And because of their respective locations, a similar status has devolved upon many of the islands and territories within it—such as Djibouti, Reunion Island, Socotra and the British Indian Ocean Territory (particularly the coral atoll of Diego Garcia).

For Australia, despite its past reluctance to seriously address the issue of Indian Ocean security, the SLOCs across it have been traditionally of the highest significance: they were, as T.B. Millar observes, the "life-line" of the Empire and of Australian trade with Britain and Western Europe.[2] With the sun now almost set on that empire, the analogy of "life-line" is still, however, appropriate, at least in terms of trade. As Table 1 shows, the Indian Ocean SLOCs account for nearly 40 per cent of all shipping movements, and over 51 per cent of the tonnage shipped to and from Australia.[3]

Additionally, Australia's Indian Ocean coastline and hinterland are among the most remote, under developed, yet resource rich regions of the country. From the largest natural resource development in Australia's history which is the North West Shelf Gas Project, to the diamond, alumina, iron ore, oil and natural gas deposits of the Kimberley, to the unique importance of the port of Darwin in the context of any large scale enemy lodgement or invasion are currently derived great economic benefit and the promise of considerably more. Their loss or lengthy interruption would constitute a disruption of serious proportions to both the domestic and overseas components of the national economy.[4] It is

TABLE 1

SHIPPING MOVEMENTS TO AND FROM AUSTRALIA 1984-85

Route	No. of Movements	Tonnage (mill. DWT)
Cape of Good Hope/South Africa	553	42.5
East Africa	51	1.0
Suez Canal/Red Sea	823	29.0
Persian Gulf/India	753	29.0
Sunda Strait	1277	32.0
Lombok Strait	288	12.4
Ombai Strait	1397	151.1
Wetar Strait	80	4.5
Total	5222	301.5
Total No. of Movements to and from Australia	13074	584.5
Percent Via Indian Ocean	39.9	51.6

not surprising, then, that the Minister for Foreign Affairs, Mr Bill Hayden, chose to redefine the Indian Ocean's position in Australia's foreign policy with a major speech in 1984 during the course of which he proposed that there were "unassailable reasons of national self-interest why the region should hold a consistent and sensible place in our scale of priorities ..."[5]

In the light of this statement and subsequent actions taken to affirm it, it is worth asking why it was that Australian policy-makers chose to neglect the Indian Ocean for so long. The answer appears to lie in what Hayden termed the "Eastern tilt"—a consequence of the extreme concentration of population in the south-east of the continent.[6] As Ball and Langtry describe it:

> The combined population of Victoria and New South Wales alone is 9.4 million. There are less than a million people north of the 26th parallel—an area almost exactly half of the Australian continent.[7]

When it is also considered that Western Australia, the largest state in the federation, has a population of just 1.5 million the demographic reflex towards neglect is as understandable as it is to be deprecated. In combination with the massive distances involved it became easy to dismiss the north and north-west as in the famous phrase, "a far away place of which we know nothing". And the comparisons made by Ball and Langtry are illuminating:

> Irian Jaya is only 150 miles across the Torres Strait from Bamaga at the tip of the Cape York Peninsula. *Australia's north-west coastline is closer to the South China Sea, and to Vietnam, than it is to the Tasman Sea.* Broome [in Western Australia's north-west] is approximately equidistant from Canberra and Bangkok and Manila, *and is actually closer to the other three ASEAN capitals of Jakarta, Singapore and Kuala Lumpur than it is to Canberra.* (emphasis added)[8]

In global strategic terms neglect was reinforced by the agreeable strategic character of the Indian Ocean until 1968. Britain, to this time, held a strong position while the Soviet Union's naval presence was spasmodic, for purposes of transit, and lacking in permanence. In this period, however, Britain first announced, and then implemented its withdrawal from east of the Suez Canal, while the Soviet Union changed its attention to a more permanent one. And both of these developments coincided with the resource-based economic growth of Western Australia and an initial response to them by the United States which tended to downplay the Soviet initiative.[9]

With the passage of time, and as events throughout the "arc of instability" dictated, both Australia and the United States came to conclusions which now act as the basis of their respective policies.[10] For Australia, a dependent member of the US system of alliances, a certain commonality of interests with the US was implied and these, too, have found a tangible expression in the country's Indian Ocean posture. Tangibility of expression, however, has not been an obvious feature of the Indian Ocean policy even since 1968; indeed, the lead time for it to have been observed in real terms at all was of the order of 14 years. Thus, despite the government's offer of Cockburn Sound to the United States, and the United States invitation to Australia to provide forces for the Rapid Deployment Force (both of which were declined) in the wake of the Soviet invasion of Afghanistan, it was not until late 1984 that a substantial resource commitment (treated later in this paper) was made.

As much as culpable negligence, the sheer size and complexity of the Indian Ocean security problem also contributed to the situation in the interim years. And the latter was intimidating: for the most part, as the introduction to this essay suggests, Australia was faced with defence and foreign policy interests and objectives which were beyond its capability to influence and achieve, respectively. It was, and remains, therefore, confronted in the Indian Ocean with a regional variant of the national security dilemma. To overcome it, Australia, somewhat naturally, has adopted a regional variant of the national security solution: it has sought to maximise its self-reliance within the bounds of perceived political tolerance and economic reality while at the same time depending on the alliance with the United States for the enhancement of security beyond its purely national capabilities. Of necessity this is a compromise solution in terms of Australian sovereignty and at times it even involves policies which are at odds with each other, if not contradictory.

Australia's attempts to address Indian Ocean issues are guided by two long-term objectives—the promotion of disarmament and the reduction of Superpower tensions. Since both are extremely dependent on factors well beyond Australia's control, a more immediate *diplomatic* approach has been formulated with three main components: the allocation of foreign aid to Indian Ocean selected states on a higher priority; the establishment of a higher Australian profile in the region; and the establishment of a Zone of Peace.[11] All three, it should be noted, reflect a certain anxiety about the problems of the region, are couched in hope rather than expectation and are no more than modest measures, modestly expressed.[12] They are, moreover, dominated by the *strategic* approach to the region which, in many of its facets, runs counter to the Zone of Peace, at least in the short term.

In relation to the re-ordering of foreign aid priorities, the government relied heavily on the findings of the Jackson Committee's **Report on Australia's Overseas Aid Programme**.[13] This found that India in particular should rank more highly as an aid recipient than hitherto and it also proposed that the island states of the Indian Ocean be placed in the highest of the four geographic categories of aid on the basis of both their special regional importance to Australia and the nature of their problems. The latter are, in many ways, similar to the constraints on development which affect islands in the South Pacific and are, therefore, familiar to Australia and amenable to the bilateral programmes devised in that area.[14]

Notwithstanding this declaratory policy, the translation of the promise of the Jackson Committee's report into actual aid remains largely unfulfilled. As of 1987, no major shifts in the distribution of official development assistance (ODA) hasd taken place. In fact, the ODA programmes of 1985-87 and 1986-87 reflected what the government termed its "reduced capacity to provide assistance due to the urgent need to curb the level of real government spending".[15] In particular it reflected the need to reduce pressures on the external account. Thus it was that the ODA programme, as a percentage of Gross National Product, has undergone a steady decline in the years 1984-87—from 0.50 per cent in 1984-85 to 0.39 per cent in 1986-87.

Within this straitened fiscal climate the Jackson Committee's Indian Ocean recommendations, quoted so approvingly in 1984, became casualties. India failed to feature in either of the two subsequent ODA programmes while the island states received, first, $6.3 million, and then $5 million. In the 1986-87 ODA Report the Indian Ocean was conspicuous by its absence from the opening statement of priorities, having seemingly been displaced by the needs of post-revolution Philippines.[16] This is not to say that the re-ordering of aid priorities recommended by the Jackson Committee will not eventuate, but rather that, in aid terms, the diplomatic approach to the Indian Ocean's problems awaits a measure of substance.

The lack of appropriations for India requires a further brief mention. In Hayden's 1984 speech on the Indian Ocean, he mystified both a large number of his listeners and not a few defence and foreign policy analysts by emphasising India as an "obviously special case, for various significant reasons." These reasons, as adumbrated, were overwhelmingly strategic and couched in terms that denoted a somewhat vague uneasiness. Over four years later, the Foreign Minister's pre-occupation has still not been adequately accounted for. Furthermore, if India is a economically strong as Hayden proclaimed any Australian aid would seem to be unnecessary or at least without the priority he accorded it. Possibly, however, Hayden was reflecting not so much an Australian concern as an ASEAN cocern—in particular, Indonesian perceptions that India's growing capabilities imply intentions of regional dominance. For this reason and because neither the magnitude nor the direction of the Indian military build-up can any longer be left undiscussed in an enterprise of the nature of this conference, it is necessary to digress briefly on the immediate changes that are taking place in the armed services of the region's (and the world's) largest functioning democracy. Such a digression is, moreover, undertaken with due acknowledgement of the dictum that capabilities need not necessarily imply intentions.

For some years now strategic analysts have observed the development of Indian military capability to the point where, by the late 1970s, the country possessed the world's third largest standing army (1.1 million personnel) and fifth largest air force. While both of these attracted comment that this represented a measure of over-deterrence in terms of India's likely adversaries, it is the current burgeoning of the navy which shapes and focuses speculation and an embryonic uneasiness. When the Foreign Minister gave his address he referred to the ranking of the Indian Navy as the eighth largest: such has been the rate of acquisition in this service that, in 1987, it overtook Italy's 108,000 ton navy (7th largest) by 50,000 tons, and by the end of 1988 will almost certaintly displace West Germany's 170,000 ton fleet from 6th place. Only the two superpowers and Britain, France and Japan will have bigger fleets.

For a country whose perennial concerns have been induced by regional-continental neighbours, this is something of a radical departure. After three land wars with Pakistan and one border war with China over the last 41 years, and the adoption and development of non-alignment as a foreign policy posture, the array of Indian capabilities suggests power projection and sea-denial in the arc which extends from South Africa to Australia. In complexion the navy is moving from frigates, destroyers and diesel-powered submarines which are consistent with purely national defence and a 7,500 km (4,700 mile) coastline, to nuclear-powered submarines and modern attack aircraft carriers found only in blue-water navies. And while this writer would be the first to concede that tonnage is but a crude indicator and might, as well, correlate weakly, or not at all with quality, it is nevertheless difficult to formulate negative propositions in this regard. By many accepted standards India is a powerful and vital country: it is a successful producer of oil, iron ore and thorium. In terms of Gross National Product it is in the top 10 of the world's economies, i.e. within more-a-less the same "league" as its military capabilities. Significantly, when considering quality it has a university population in excess of four million, and consequently an extremely large pool of trained professional, scientific, technological and executive talent. Thus for quality within the armed services not to have improved with expansion, a case would need to be made which posits, contrary to reasonable inference, separate rates of development as between the military and civilian sectors of Indian society whereby the former is markedly inferior.

The new sea-denial and power projection capabilities in any case demand qualitative improvement because of the very nature of the individual systems in question—naval aviation and nuclear maritime power—and the added requirements which will be made as a result of carrier group operations. From 1991, therefore, when India starts to deploy the first of its Soviet "Sierra" class SSNs, the Indian Ocean littoral states are likely to be even more questioning than they are now and certainly more demanding of answers from a country which is already South Asia's pre-eminent military power.

As regards the second component of the diplomatic approach, a higher Australian profile in the region, the commitment has been more apparent in financial terms with $120 million in aid flowing to *Africa* in the years 1984-1986. In terms of the Indian Ocean island states however, the principal feature was the establishment of permanent Australian diplomatic representation in Mauritius (with oversight responsibilities in the other island states) and the institution of a programme of regular naval visits through the region. The latter took effect in mid-1984 with a visit by HMAS *Brisbane* to Sri Lanka, Maldives, Seychelles and Kenya.

That this diplomatic initiative should be undertaken by a unit of the Australian Defence Forces highlights both the limits to the diplomatic approach and the tension between it and the strategic approach. In particular, it points to the ambivalence which surrounds the third component of Australia's regional diplomacy -the establishment of an "Indian Ocean Peace Zone", promoted mainly by Sri Lanka. Australian enthusiasm for such an arrangement originated with the Whitlam Government of 1972-75, motivated in part by Labor's expressed greater sympathy for the causes espoused by the Afro-Asian world, but also by what T.B. Millar described as the "irreproachable" nature of the objective and the extremely remote possibility that, even if it were unlikely to be fully achieved, it might possibly facilitate a regional ceiling on superpower arms.[17] To these ends Australia obtained foundation membership of the relevant United Nations organ designed to implement the zone of peace, the Ad Hoc Committee on the Indian Ocean, and subsequently became chairman of the Western Group of Nations involved in it.

To date, the Zone of Peace remains an aspiration, no closer and perhaps further from realisation than when it was first proposed, in 1964. In the period since the Whitlam Government embraced it, the succession of conservative coalition governments under Malcolm Fraser rejected both it and most of the rationale for Australia's regional approach in the Indian Ocean. The residual component was the desirability of a balance of forces between the superpowers at the lowest possible level, and this was elevated, not the least by Fraser himself, to the cornerstone of Australian Indian Ocean policy.[18]

In the light of the foregoing it might seem to have been incumbent upon Australia, between 1975 and 1983, to have surrendered its seat on the Ad Hoc Committee, but it did not. Despite the fact that the Fraser Governments of this period rejected the Indian Ocean Peace Zone as impractical, they also came to understand the wider implications of the principle *les absent ont toujours tort* and concluded that the costs of exit were uncomfortable (and even costly) isolation and the almost certain loss of influence which accrued from membership of the Committee.[19] As Millar observes of this ambivalence, it tends, in the final analysis towards hypocrisy.[20]

Hypocrisy was, in any case, an established basis of Australian policy long before 1975, largely because of the aforementioned dominance of the stategic, over the diplomatic approach to Indian Ocean issues. In justice, though it must be conceded that the nature of the issues makes some taint of compromise inescapable: Australia is faced with an immediate problem—security—which requires immediate measures, yet none of them are as compelling, intellectually speaking, as the long-term objectives which would render all other expedients redundant. The difficulty for

Australia, as for other nations in similar positions, lies in the accommodations which must be reached when the requirements of the long-term objective necessitate radical transformations of power relationships which are beyond the country's ability to effect. And in an international political system which has elevated to the status of virtue the integration of power, morality and self-interest under the practice of *realpolitik*, hypocrisy is not without the appeal of an imperative. That what is being practised is essentially a flawed virtue is thought not to prevail over its otherwise redeeming features; indeed, the latter are held to be sufficient to challenge the very notion that "practical politics" or the pursuit of the "policy of the possible" is, or should be, morally and politically repugnant. The imputation of hypocrisy, then, is tendentious, but arguable in terms of the strategic approach Australia has adopted to the Indian Ocean.

As regards the provision of purely national resources, Australian governments, as noted earlier, were extraordinarily tardy until the mid 1980s. Although signals intelligence facilities concerned with the Indian Ocean region existed as early as 1946 in Western Australia, it was not until August 1984 that strike elements of the Australian Defence Force were designated, on a permanent basis, for regional security roles which related *inter alia* to the Indian Ocean. In that month it was announced that the RAAF would be locating its 75 Squadron, with the new FA/18 tactical fighter, at Tindal, near Katherine in the Northern Territory. This expensive (in excess of A$240 million over the first five years, in 1984 dollar terms) project is, however, to be seen not only in Indian Ocean terms but also in the context of the development of northern defence from Learmonth and Derby in the north-west, through Darwin and Tindal in the north, to Weipa and Townsville in the north-east, in conjunction with the JINDALEE over-the-horizon-radar system.

Subsequently, a 1985 statement named Cockburn Sound as the new home-port for some of the Royal Australian Navy's (RAN) fleet of six ageing Oberon class submarines, thus preparing the way for the eventual west-coast basing of the entire submarine fleet. But more importantly, the **Review of Australia's Defence Capabilities** (undertaken by Paul Dibb) of March 1986 and the Defence White Paper tabled 12 months later provided the rationale and extent to which the Indian Ocean dimension of Australia's security was a priority concern.[21] Within a concept known as "greater defence self-reliance" policies were announced consistent with, but in scope far beyond the decisions of 1984-85.

In addition to measures already covered, a considerably increased Army presence in the north of Australia was announced as was a limited naval facility on the north-west coast and a substantial new intelligence facilty at Geraldton, to be operated by the Defence Signals Directorate. The most radical development, however, concerned the decision to transform the RAN into a two-ocean navy with half of the fleet to be based at HMAS *Stirling*, near Perth, complementing the redeployment of the submarine force. In time-on-station alone the move, which admittedly will be staged over 10 years, will increase the effectiveness of destroyer types by 13 per cent and submarines by 31 per cent.

While this initiative met with widespread approval it should be noted in passing that it gives rise to two reservations. The first concerns whether or not splitting what was, effectively, not substantially more than a one-ocean navy until 1987, into two constituent parts, warrants use of the term "two-ocean navy". The second is financial and concerns the strength of purpose of Australian governments to adequately finance the transformation under way during times in which a reduction in defence spending might appear to be expedient. And here the difference between the Dibb **Review** which was predicated on a defence outlay of around three per cent of Gross Domestic Product (GDP) and a slightly higher figure for annual real growth, and the Defence White Paper, which posits that the defence programme can be afforded *without real growth* (both against a recent historical background in which three per cent of GDP has seldom obtained).[22]

Concern, too, is warranted regarding the status which will be accorded Christmas Island and the Cocos Island group, Australia's remote north-east Indian Ocean territories. Though both are thought defensible in terms of the Dibb **Review's** recommendations, there are, as Ross Babbage has argued,[23] several "direct consequences" of their status as a defence asset:

> In low and medium level contingencies, Christmas and the Cocos Islands have the potential to serve as a shield or forward line of defence on Australia's north-western approaches that would complicate an

> opponent's operations and channel his lines of approach to the mainland. Perhaps more importantly, these territories also have the potential in many circumstances to distract the opponent and force him to fight initially far offshore, rather than on the continent itself. In a period of crisis, this could buy Australia substantial time to cover national mobilisation and provide opportunities to exact a heavy toll on the opponent's high technology units.[24]

Accordingly, until such time as the defence of these islands is given detailed consideration a serious lacuna will exist in an otherwise improved Australian Indian Ocean strategy.

Implicit in the question of Christmas and the Cocos Islands is the parallel question of how to reconcile what is, for Australia, an ends-means mismatch. Stated simply, Australia has scarce defence resources, acutely so when it is realised that the *closest* of these territories (Christmas Island) is over 1400 kilometres from the nearest point on the Australian mainland and both are closer to Indonesia, Christmas Island significantly so.[25] In recognition of the fact that national efforts alone were insufficient to fasten the required level of regional security, Australia sought to extend the deterrent role of the alliance with the United States to cover the country 's western approaches as well as its Pacific environs. Though, technically the centrepoint of this alliance, the ANZUS Treaty of 1951, was not applicable to the Indian Ocean, a form of words was agreed between the signatories in February 1980 that permitted admission of the region to future treaty activities.[26] When, in July 1983, the Minister for Foreign Affairs, Bill Hayden, unilaterally but without demur, narrowed the geographic scope of ANZUS to the Pacific area and the defence of Australia the Indian Ocean appeared once more to be excluded.[27] But even this is probably not irrevocable: as Thomas D. Young concluded, the origin of a threat to Austrtalia "would make the geographic parameters of the Treaty esoteric, since it would be in all the parties'interest to meet an opposing force at the Alliance's most advantageous place and time, even if this were in mid-Indian Ocean".[28] The relevance of the Treaty to the Indian Ocean is, therefore, contingent, although the extent to which the United States is facilitated in its Indian Ocean operations by Australia would appear to give the lie to this.

For the United States, the Indian Ocean, its contiguous seas and hinterland have become priority strategic areas for all of the reasons which forced Australia to concentrate on the region *and* for the additional reason that, as a superpower, American interests are global and difficult to deny. In many aspects of their respective Indian Ocean policies, therefore, there is an identity, if not a congruence of interests. Not surprisingly, it finds its clearest expression in the support made available in the Northern Territory and Western Australia which can be categorised under three headings: hospitality, intelligence and communications.

Hospitality translates most easily to ship visits, mainly to the port of Fremantle and the RAN facilities in Cockburn Sound. The vessels involved cover a wide range of types—from aircraft carriers and their escorts to nuclear-powered, attack/hunter-killer submarines. Although there are minor fluctuations in the numbers of surface combatants, and major fluctuations in the numbers of submarines, this arrangement has brought, on average, over 30,000 US naval personnel in 42 vessels per year since 1982. (The major fluctuation in submarines, down from an average of approximately one per month in the period 1980-March 1982, to one every two months in the period March 1982-December 1985, to just one in 1986, is explained by the changing nature of USN naval deployments in the Indian and Pacific Oceans in these years, and consequently, the regional requirement for attack/hunter-killer submarines.

Within the scope of the ship visits programme, exercises are also held which provide US forces with opportunities not normally available away from their permanent bases. In the Lancelin area north of Perth firing of live ammunition is permitted in the course of amphibious exercises. This facilitates a level of operational reality for US forces unique in a span of the earth's surface which extends westward from US bases in the North Pacific to the mid Mediterranean.

More significant than such visits is the support lent to the United States for the purpose of gathering signals intelligence. In this effort Australia both contributes nationally generated intelligence and provides certain resources and rights for use by the United States. In relation to the former, the Defence Signals Directorate (DSD) operates a unit at Royal Australian Air Force Base, Pearce (near Perth), for the principal purpose of monitoring naval and air traffic over the Indian Ocean as part of a world wide system of ocean surveillance operated by the United States Navy.

In addition DSD also operates a similar establishment at Shoal Bay in the Northern Territory with responsibility for Southeast Asia, and hence, of relevance to the Indian Ocean.[29] As regards the latter support, the Australian Government, in February 1980, granted the United States Air Force (USAF) overflight rights for B-52s engaged in low-level navigation flights. Subsequently, in March 1981, an agreement between Canberra and Washington extended the nature of this arrangement to "unarmed" B-52 flights engaged in navigation training and sea surveillance operations in the Indian Ocean area. Within the scope of this agreement USAF support aircraft, and associated equipment and personnel are deployed periodically to Darwin while the B-52s themselves received staging rights through RAAF Base Darwin.[30]

Of a higher level of importance still is the third category of support, communications—in particular the Naval Communications Station, Harold E. Holt, on the North West Cape of Western Australia. Although this facility serves several purposes—indeed it performs important signals intelligence functions—its primary role is to provide a Very Low Frequency communications link with the Fleet Ballistic Missile (FBM) and attack submarine fleet of the US Navy in the Indian Ocean and the western and southern Pacific Ocean. It therefore services that part of the strategic triad which the United States regards as its most invulnerable nuclear deterrent. Since September 1982, however, North West Cape has undergone, perhaps only temporarily, a change in importance insofar as the US Navy is concerned. As of that time, its role of communicating with FBM submarines has been superseded by two facilities on each side of the US mainland.[31]

Nevertheless it remains fully capable of resuming its original mission; in the meantime, its submarine communications are in relation to the USN's attack submarines and the submarines of the RAN.

In a much less direct manner, Australia has also supported the transformation of Diego Garcia from something of an ornament amongst Britain's strategic assets to a US facility of crucial importance in the region. Its advantages are numerous and derive from its geographic location 1600 kilometres south of the tip of India and 3220 kilometres east of Africa. It is, at the same time "ideally situated for monitoring naval traffic in the Indian Ocean" and a permanent and substantial establishment for the prepositioning and provisioning of long-term support for the US Central Command (formerly the Rapid Deployment Force).[32] In potential, too, it is rich—including as a forward base for FBM submarines carrying the Trident D-5 missile (under a different USN doctrine than now operates), and as a ground-based terminal for a new system designed to provide enhanced detection of Soviet anti-satellite weapons.[33]

For Australia, the transformation of Diego Garcia since 1971, when US construction teams arrived, presented a dilemma of the type likely to be regarded as hypocrisy in its attempted resolution. Initially, US proposals to expand the island into a major forward base were given a critical reception by the Whitlam Government, but in the realisation that alliance interests were prejudiced by the presence of the Soviet Navy in the Indian Ocean, it was accepted. Accepted in an ambivalent fashion that is: the first reaction was publicly expressed while the second was more private, and based on a preference for the "lowest practical" level of force.[34] In the years since this accommodation the strategic development of Diego Garcia has proceeded without Australian objections.

The only remaining area of alliance co-operation in the Indian Ocean worthy of note is an arrangement covering the air defence of Malaysia and Singapore under the Five Power Defence Arrangements.[35] Basically this agreement is a remnant from another era when Britain was deployed east of Suez and Australia and New Zealand practised "forward defence". In the late 1980s this situation manifestly does not apply and so the Arrangements, insofar as the two countries at the "gateway" to the Indian Ocean are concerned, rest on little more than local capabilities and the resources of Australia. The extent of assistance in time of crisis, however, is neither specified nor promised although, given the strategic priorities involved, it is unlikely that Australia could refuse a request to counter a threat which eventually might be directed against its immediate northern and western interests.

For most of Australia's history as an independent country the Indian Ocean has existed more as a geographical expression than an international political and strategic reality. Even when the region was understood in such terms Australia's strategic policy appeared to take its inspiration, not from Alfred Thayer Mahan, as might be expected, but from a medieval Italian poet. To this extent the Indian Ocean was a standing reproach to the concept of rational policy-making as it was practised in Canberra. When understanding finally proceeded from urgency, policies remained so bereft of substance that they could not be seen as other than an illogical inference from the objective circumstances as they were understood. In strategic folly (as in literary chic) Dante's admonition was, by 1984, superseded by a measure of wisdom in Indian Ocean matters. To be sure, this is a wisdom which is redolent with strategic concern over all others; indeed, it is barely solvent in its holistic content. But in terms of the attitudes which prevailed until recently it is a beginning. And, though late, it is at least an acknowledgement of the principle that significant objects, or things ignored for too long, rarely return unavenged.

The academic, of course, reaches such judgements with a somewhat troubled mind. The enticement of an opportunity to exercise one's expository skills on a matter of grand strategy, and before an informed audience, is compromised by the very breathtaking sweep of the subject at hand and the uncertainties attendant on discussing it in a period of time more appropriately measured in minutes. But more than that, insofar as Australia is concerned, it results from an inkling that older, inappropriate molds of thought which could be almost instinctively criticised, held in contempt, and gracefully dismissed, have been broken. Thus a certain analytical discomfort is induced by the new lack of definition and the observation made by William V. Shannon, former United States Ambassador to Ireland, is recalled, partly as a corrective, partly in consolation:

> Nothing is so frustrating as a bad situation that is beginning to improve.

NOTES

1. Iqbal Singh, "Indian Ocean: a Zone of Peace or Power Play?", Working Paper No. 64 (Canberra: Strategic and Defence Studies Centre, Australian National University, 1982), pp.1-7.
2. T.B. Millar, **Australia In Peace and War** (Canberra: Australian National University Press, 1978), p.357.
3. Department of Defence (Navy Office), "An Analysis of Trends in Trade and Shipping", Department of Defence, Canberra, November 1985. Unfortunately the value and weight tables

do not allow for separate Indian Ocean figures to be distinguished, and heavy reliance, therefore, must be placed on shipping movements data. The percentages obtained with that data are, however, sensitive to the inclusion of the Ombai and Wetar Straits movements which only use the extreme northeast corner of the Indian Ocean, ie the northwest resource ports (mainly Port Hedland) to the archipelago. The relatively high tonnage for Ombai Strait reflects the type of ship using that route (large ore carriers) and distorts the percentate figure for tonnage using the Indian Ocean.

4. J.O. Langtry and Desmond Ball (eds), **Vulnerable Country?: Civil Resources in the Defence of Australia** (Canberra: Strategic and Defence Studies Centre, Australian National University, 1986), pp.114-218 (hereafter cited as Langtry and Ball, **A Vulnerable Country?**).

5. Speech by the Minister for Foreign Affairs, Mr Bill Hayden, MP, on the subject of the Indian Ocean, delivered to the Australian Institute of International Affairs in Perth on 20 June 1984, p.A3. The full text of this speech is found in Department of Foreign Affairs, **Backgrounder,** No. 436, 27 June 1984, pp.A1-A15 (hereafter cited as Hayden, "Indian Ocean" Speech).

6. Ibid., p.A2.

7. Langtry and Ball, **A Vulnerable Country?**, p.569.

8. Ibid.

9. Kim C. Beazley and Ian Clark, **The Politics of Intrusion: The Superpowers and the Indian Ocean** (Sydney: Alternative Publishing Cooperative, 1979), pp.127-43.

10. Henry S. Albinski, "Australia and the Indian Ocean", Larry W. Bowman and Ian Clark (eds), **The Indian Ocean in Global Politics** (Nedlands, WA: University of Western Australia Press, 1981), pp.59-86.

11. Hayden, "Indian Ocean" Speech, p.A9.

12. Ibid., pp.A9-A13.

13. See Joint Committee on Foreign Affairs and Defence, The Parliament of the Commonwealth of Australia, **The Jackson Report on Australia's Overseas Aid Program** (Canberra: Australian Government Publishing Service, 1985).

14. Hayden, "Indian Ocean" Speech, p.A10.
15. Australia's Overseas Development Assistant Program 1986-87, 1986-87 Budget Paper No. 9 (Canberra: Australian Government Publishing Service, 1986), p.1.
16. Ibid.
17. Millar, op.cit., pp.412-13.
18. Dieter Braun, **The Indian Ocean: Region of Conflict or Peace Zone?** (Canberra: Croom Helm, 1983), pp.116-17.
19. Les Absent Ont Toujours Tort (Fr.) The absent are always wrong (or in the wrong).
20. Millar, op.cit., p.426.
21. See **Review of Australia's Defence Capabilities,** Report to the Minister for Defence by Mr Paul Dibb (Canberra: Australian Government Publishing Service, 1986), hereafter cited as the Dibb **Review**; and "Tabling Statement, Defence Policy Information Paper—19 March 1987", by the Minister for Defence Mr Kim C. Beazley, MP, issued by the National Media Liaison Service.
22. Dibb **Review**, pp.16 and 160-76.
23. Ibid., p.15.
24. Ross Babbage, "Christmas and the Cocos Islands: Defence Liabilities or Assets?" pp.41-2, draft of Part 5 of **The Defence of Northern Australia** (forthcoming). The writer is grateful to Dr Babbage of the Strategic and Defence Studies Centre, Australian National University, for making this paper available.
25. Ibid., pp.2 and 16.
26. Braun, op.cit., p.121.
27. Ramesh Thakur, **In Defence of New Zealand: Foreign Policy Choices in the Nuclear Age** (Boulder: Westview, 1986), p.99.
28. Thomas D. Young, "ANZUS in the Indian Ocean: Strategic Considerations", memoir presented for the Diploma of the University Institute of Advanced International Studies, Geneva, 1982, p.4, as cited in Henry S. Albinski, "Australia, New Zealand, and Indian Ocean Security: Perspectives and

Contributions from Outlying American Alliance Partners", William L. Dowdy and Russell B. Trood (eds), **The Indian Ocean: Perspectives on a Strategic Arena** (Durham: Duke University Press, 1985), p.359.

29. Jeffrey T. Richelson and Desmond Ball, **The Ties that Bind: Intelligence Cooperation Between the UKUSA Countries—United Kingdom, The United States of America, Canada, Australia and New Zealand** (Boston: Allen and Unwin, 1985), pp.192-3, and 208-9.

30. Desmond Ball and J.O. Langtry (eds), **Civil Defence and Australia's Security in the Nuclear Age** (Canberra: Strategic and Defence Studies Centre, Australian National University, 1983), p.155

31. For a detailed analysis of the North West Cape facility see Desmond Ball, **A Suitable Piece of Real Estate: American Installations in Australia** (Sydney: Hale and Iremonger, 1980), pp.50-57. A brief account of the changed status of the facility is found in William Pinwill, "Capes deterrence role at end", **National Times**, 4-10 July 1986, p.24.

32. Richelson and Ball, op.cit., pp.202, 204-6, and Larry W. Bowman and Jeffrey A. Lefebvre, "The Indian Ocean: US Military and Strategic Perspectives", Dowdy and Trood (eds), op.cit., pp.422-25.

33. Robert C. Aldridge, **First Strike!: The Pentagon's Strategy for Nuclear War** (London: Pluto, 1983), pp.82-3 and 215-16.

34. Millar, op.cit., p.418.

35. See Chin Kin Wah, **The Defence of Malaysia and Singapore: The Transformation of a Security System 1957-1971** (Cambridge: Cambridge University Press, 1983), pp.144-178.

Comments

Hugh Collins

I propose to raise in summary fashion three points which emerge very clearly from Dr McKinley's paper, and then to consider three questions I have about issues arising from his contentions and observations.

First, on the Indian Ocean as a region requiring strategic analysis, I think that Dr McKinley introduces a most interesting question. He asks whether the Indian Ocean is better understood as a collection of sub-regions than a single region. An exploration of the political phenomena underlying that question would lead us fruitfully into many of the policy dilemmas that this seminar must consider. When one recalls that in international politics a region may be defined by a dominant conflict rather than by effective cooperation, Dr McKinley's question is worth pondering.

Secondly, I was impressed by Dr McKinley's assertion that "for most of Australia's history as an independent country the Indian Ocean has existed more as a geographical expression than an international political and strategic reality". His paper provides a useful review of the Indian Ocean in Australian policy. This he treats largely as a history of neglect: purblind, irrational, free-loading neglect, indeed. The twin explanations for this he finds in strategy (the Indian Ocean has been a relatively benign strategic environment for most of the period he is criticising) and demography (it is far removed from the major concentrations of populations). The latter point turns out to be a reflection not so much of where people lived, but of where most Australians voted. Yet we should note that during the period about which Dr McKinley is so critical of Australian policy towards the Indian Ocean region, a number of very prominent Western Australian politicians held the relevant portfolios of Defence and External/Foreign Affairs. Does this suggest a mismatch between the thrust of their policies and what Dr McKinley or others might describe as their immediate interests? Or does it testify to the strength of the underlying strategic perceptions, held by leaders from the isolated southwestern as well as the populous southeastern corner of the continent? It has taken until Mr

Beazley for half the fleet to come to the protection of the federal division of Swan: this shift in the disposition of naval resources is a major shift in strategic perceptions. Does this amount to a clear reversal of the history which Dr McKinley has reviewed for us?

Thirdly, the paper deals with the most recent developments in Australian policy, noting especially the new national stake in the North-West and the change which this new resource-based economic interest has made to Australia's defence calculations. About the new defence orientation Dr McKinley asks two good questions. The first has to do with what is meant by "two ocean navy" and how that is to be distinguished from one navy divided in half. The second question is whether Australia is willing to pay for a policy of this kind. As to the first of these questions, we shall have the expositions by Admiral Robertson and others to elucidate the meaning of the developments described by the Minister. As to the second question, the Minister has not disguised the constraints affecting any government's capacity to carry through the commitments which his government has made in this area.

Having noted some of the key points to be extracted from Dr McKinley's paper, I wish to raise further questions in three areas. One set of questions concerns defence policy; a second set has to do with domestic politics; the third relates to connections between foreign and defence policies.

First, defence policy issues. What will be the impact in policy-making of the changes set out in the Defence White Paper and elaborated for us in such detail in Mr Beazley's paper? We have yet to see the effect upon those who make policy of a substantial, permanent concentration of force on the western shores of this nation. What will be the impact upon the forces themselves, upon their ideas about their mission, about their procurement policies, about their strategic environment, once they adjust to very different relationships and operational bases? Current policy raises some very large and interesting questions of this kind. Perhaps Dr McKinley's imminent translation to Canberra can be seen as part of that redressing of the balance of "southeastern" dominance in Australian policy which the recent policy changes portend more generally.

Secondly, some domestic political issues. What will be the domestic political consequences of the 1987 defence policy decisions? I believe that Dr McKinley is right to point to the alteration in the assessment of the Australian national interest which the major developments in the north-west of this country have brought about. One could go on to point out that those who were largely responsible for the development of the North-West's resources rarely gave defence a thought. This vast economic development occurred chiefly under the aegis of State leaders who bore no responsibility for the thinking through its impact upon defence, let alone its contribution towards defence.

As a new theatre of interest, the Indian Ocean underlines the fact that Australia's defence contingencies have become an interesting study in the politics of federalism. Indeed, the more people talk about lower levels of our defence contingencies as messy, nasty, local situations, the more they are describing situations requiring a combination of military and police action. This will involve close attention to the integration of responsibilities and agencies at State and Commonwealth levels.So there are some very interesting administrative and political questions and issues on our western horizon. The sheer movement of personnel, with the attendant provision of infrastructure, of housing, education and health services; the benefits being argued—and anticipated—in increased local consumption: we have yet to fully analyze the domestic political consequences of these decisions.

We can also expect that there will be domestic political conflict. Those aspects of the relationship with the United States that Dr McKinley usefully summarises as hospitality, intelligence and communications will all be the focus of protest. Articulate and politically-sensitive citizens in this State will challenge these activities. These challenges will largely relate to issues well beyond the scope of the Indian Ocean region, so those who seek to analyze these alliance functions primarily in relation to regional roles will have to tackle a domestic political critique that may be based upon radically different criteria and assumptions.

Finally, the connections between foreign and defence policies. In introducing his valuable paper, the Minister for Defence remarked that he would keep to his ministerial brief and avoid straying into the policy domains of cabinet colleagues. This assurance was presumably aimed more at those colleagues than at this conference, despite Mr Beazley's confidence that this Seminar's discussions would fill in any gaps. Yet it is the squaring of the defence and the diplomatic aspects of policy in this area which poses the most contentious and difficult aspect of these problems. One need look no further for an example of such difficulties than Dr McKinley's caustic observations on Australia's declaratory policy towards the Indian Ocean Zone of Peace.

One of the problems facing us, I think, is that, just as it may be asked whether or not the Indian Ocean region turns out to be a collection of sub-regions, so one may ask whether many of the questions which arise in this region are secondary to other issues about which we have primary concerns. Indeed, I think this makes the frequent assertion of the strategic primacy of the Indian Ocean open to challenge.

This does not mean that regional issues are unimportant. Rather, it is to say that they arise typically in a secondary fashion, or have to be considered alongside other issues. This is simply to say that regional questions have to be assessed from both global and national perspectives. For example, an issue which has received little attention in the discussion so far is the impact of nuclear proliferation in the region. This is a policy issue of major global and national significance. It will have important consequences for the region, but its impact will extend well outside this area.

Michael McKinley has graphically portrayed the partial and inadequate assessment of the Indian Ocean region in an earlier phase of Australian policy. It will be a serious shortcoming if that assessment is replaced—at least in this State—by a no less partial and inadequate view of the total requirements of Australian defence and diplomacy. With a two ocean policy and two ocean set of policy dilemmas, the challenge will be to achieve a national definition of policy and priorities. To achieve that goal, we shall have to take into account the complexities of our domestic structure as well as the complexities of the region.

Comments

Peter Reeves

There is an important question and it is the one touched on by Hugh Collins. He commented that while there had been West Australian Ministers for Defence and Foreign Affairs in previous governments, they had not ever done anything to implement a "two ocean" naval policy. But I do not think that it is the fact that Mr Beazley is a West Australian which makes the difference now. I think that what we are seeing is actually the beginnings of a fundamental shift in Australian attitudes to foreign policy, a shift in the power of the Sydney/Melbourne financial axis to dictate foreign policy. The "peripheral states", as they are sometimes called, are beginning finally to exert some power within the Federation on these kinds of issues; and Western Australia is very much to the fore in that. In the past these questions have been very much settled in the citadels of power of the Labor Party and the Liberal Party in the eastern states. Up to—and even after—the Second World War, we were oriented towards the Pacific because we felt secure in other parts of the world and because we could play a role in the South Pacific that greatly bolstered our image of ourselves. We were "big" people in New Guinea and in the islands of the Pacific; in other areas it has always been much more difficult for Australia to look credible as a "power". We have had to overcome the effects of that kind of historical orientation which has been dictated to us by our eastern seaboard population and the commercial and financial dominance of that population. It is only in the last 15 to 20 years that we've begun to see the underlying changes in attitudes which would enable us to do things other than those which the Pacific orientation of old has allowed in the past. That is the reason, I believe, why it is important to look at the questions raised in this seminar. We at the Centre hoped, for the outset, that what we would do is to raise this question about a two ocean naval *policy* (not just a question about a two ocean *navy*).

The significant question, I think, is not whether we have got at the present time a proper two ocean navy or whether we have done all that we need to do. The significant point is that we've begun to change our views and that we've begun, therefore, to face up to the responsibilities that we have in the region and that we have begun to understand the need for Australia to match its physical presence in the region with a genuine commitment to the region. We now actually have to work out how to understand the policies of major powers in a region of this size and complexity; we have to actually begin to begin with larger neighbours who are independent and who have the capability of responding to us quite directly as major actors on a world stage on which we have a more minor role. We have to learn to live with that new situation: that is the important historical element in the change that we have seen.

CHAPTER 3

The 1987 Defence White Paper—A Maritime Perspective*

A.J. Robertson

Up to about 25 years ago most travelling Australians did so by sea. They acquired a broad knowledge of shipping, ports and maritime affairs generally, together with an understanding of the importance to Australia of seaborne trade and of its unimpeded passage upon the highways of the oceans around us.

The advent of large passenger aircraft, and particularly the wide-bodied jet, spelt the end for the great passenger liners, and changed some national perceptions.

Passengers, encased in the speeding high-flying new capsules, while aware of the attentiveness and attractiveness (or otherwise) of the cabin staff, the standard of food and films and the comfort of the flight, are now cut off from any experience of maritime activities in the ports and on the vast oceans far below. This has led to a gradual erosion of public understanding of maritime matters and of the importance to Australia of merchant shipping, which still carries over 96% of our imports and exports.

Additionally, over many years, continual disruption in the ports and coastal shipping through industrial disputes, combined with, in some cases, poor management, Government indifference and the effect of much improved road systems, resulted in a massive transfer of interstate cargo to road and rail. Except for the carriage of bulk cargoes such as oil, iron ore and alumina, a great decline took place in coastal shipping. Many shipping firms, shipyards

* The views expressed in this paper are the author's. They may not necessarily be the same as the department's.

and associated industries went to the wall, arousing little public concern in their passing.

So, gradually, what had formerly been a nation with a very maritime outlook, largely lost interest and knowledge in maritime matters. After all, there were plenty of foreign merchant ships to carry our trade. The mighty U.S. Navy, supported by the British Fleet and the security provided by the ANZUS Treaty, SEATO, and other arrangements, gave us a certain surety that all was well on the oceans of the world.

But in recent years, slow-acting but powerful and inexorable forces have been at work and the broad background to our long-term security has changed greatly. The British, with their strong Fleet, which had been so vital to our survival in our first 150 years, are long gone from our northern approaches. The U.S. is suffering economic problems and its Navy, though still probably the most powerful, if no longer the world's biggest, is fully stretched worldwide, and the long term tenure of its major base in the Philippines seems threatened.

The Soviet Navy has developed enormously in size and power and has established itself firmly in the Indian Ocean and at Camranh Bay in Vietnam. It is now about to complete its balance for all types of maritime operations by the introduction of large nuclear-powered aircraft carriers.

In merchant shipping, our own industry has waned. The famed "Red Duster" has all but disappeared from our ports, along with the flags of most of our allies, while those of many nations are now to be seen including many from the Eastern Bloc. The Soviet Union has, since 1945, built a large, technologically-advanced and capable merchant marine, and the world's largest fishing fleet. These vessels are centrally controlled and are equipped to support Soviet Fleet operations when required. This was demonstrated vividly in 1986, when a number of Soviet merchant ships arrived quickly on the scene to support and tow a damaged Soviet nuclear-powered submarine in mid-Atlantic—with little regard for commercial considerations.

The scene has changed more than this, however. A number of navies in The Indian and Pacific Oceans, including those of China, Japan, India and Indonesia have undergone considerable expansion and modernisation in recent years, and must now be taken into account in the overall strategic balance.

No longer are the oceans of the world largely western-controlled lakes, as they had been for the past 4 decades.

The Chinese Navy, centred now on some 117 submarines (including 3 nuclear-powered boats) and 53 destroyers and frigates, has modernised and expanded greatly in recent years. It demonstrated its capability for long-range deployment during inter-continental ballistic missile (ICBM) firings into the South Pacific some years ago and last year carried out a large-scale naval exercise involving 70 ships in the South China Sea.

In 1987 China was reported to have approved a modernisation plan calling for the addition of more nuclear-powered submarines together with destroyers, frigates, and even aircraft carriers. The aim behind this massive programme seems to be to make China's navy one of the world's more powerful, dominant in the region, and a major force in the Pacific.

The Japanese Maritime Self Defence Force (Navy) has 15 modern submarines and 52 destroyers and frigates. It seems set for further considerable expansion as Japan, faced with increasing American pressure to take on more of its own defence responsibility, increases the percentage of its G.N.P. devoted to defence. Japan has announced its intention to defend the shipping lanes out to 1,000 nautical miles from its ports.

The Indonesian Fleet, modest in size though recently modernised, has 3 submarines and 15 frigates/corvettes. It has recently announced a massive shipbuilding programme of 23 frigates.

But perhaps the most dramatic increase in naval capability is that of India, which seems bent on creating one of the world's more powerful fleets, the reason for which has been the subject of conjecture. Such a capability seems hardly a requirement in any confrontation with Pakistan or even with China.

When Australia declined the British offer of the capable though aged aircraft-carrier H.M.S. Hermes, of Falklands War fame, the ship was purchased cheaply by India, which now has 2 aircraft-carriers (Vikrant and Hermes) equipped with Sea Harrier jump-jets and modern helicopters. A third carrier, to be built in India, appears to be under consideration, though it may possibly replace Vikrant. The Indian Navy also has 29 destroyers, frigates, and corvettes, and 11 submarines, shortly to be joined by its first

Soviet built nuclear-powered submarine. By 1995 a further 3 Soviet built guided-missile cruisers, 30 destroyers, frigates, and corvettes and 16 other vessels are due to join the fleet. Except for the carriers and a number of British-designed frigates, most vessels are Soviet-built or of Soviet design built in India. Their fleet is well supported by tankers, minesweepers and other vessels, and new naval bases are under construction in India and in the Andaman, Nicobar and Lacadive islands. Additionally, India has now formed two regiments of marines with a capable force of amphibious ships.

All of the above nations are our friends, though not our allies, today, and pose no current threat. Clearly this a most favourable situation which we must strive to preserve. But it must be remembered that "threat" is normally composed of two elements—capability and intention.

Maritime capability takes many years to acquire, but intention and alignments can change rapidly as we have often seen in international affairs. We may have little control over such events.

If the capability for long range projection of power is possessed by any nation in the Indian or Pacific Oceans, we must take note of its possible future use and effects.

In contrast, the relative power of the Royal Australian Navy from being arguably the most modern, and having the greatest power projection capability, among the local navies of the Indian and Pacific Oceans (except for the U.S. and U.S.S.R.), has declined markedly in the last ten years. The controversial decision in 1982 not to replace the aircraft-carrier H.M.A.S. Melbourne, and to sell the long range Skyhawk fighter/strike (equipped with in-flight refuelling) and Tracker anti-submarine aircraft, drastically reduced the Navy's capability.

From a force of two aircraft carriers and 42 destroyers, frigates and corvette/minesweepers twenty years ago, it has changed to a force with admittedly better base facilities and more support ships and patrol boats, but much less fighting strength represented by 12 destroyers and frigates, 6 submarines, and 3 minehunters/minesweepers—dependent (except for some ship-borne helicopters) on shore-based air support.

Recently, steps have been taken to replace the submarines, to replace and to augment somewhat the aged frigate, mine-countermeasures and helicopters forces. However, no move has been made to really strengthen the fleet with some form of integrated air power and a major increase in submarine and sealift/amphibious capability.

While the new submarines, which will not be with the fleet for many years yet, will be a major improvement in capability on the old Oberon class and will be at the forefront of technology for conventional boats, they cannot compare in many areas with nuclear-powered vessels.

Indeed, the lack of nuclear submarines in our Navy must mean that the capability of our own anti-submarine warfare forces will steadily decline for want of adequate training against the more capable nuclear boats.

There seems a strong argument to move away from the "replacement" policy of the past.

This is not to suggest that we should try to keep pace in naval power with the major nations in our north, but it is to suggest that we must ensure we can act decisively in our own defence, including ensuring a balanced, modern and effective fleet with a strong deterrent element and capable, with the Air Force, of dealing with any threat that can be deployed to our general area.

The current relative weakness of the R.A.N. must also be taken into account in any strategic consideration of the changing political realities in the S.W. Pacific where the collapse of ANZUS as a 3-power treaty, the Fijian coup, and instability in some other island groups have changed the scene in our own front garden.

It is against this maritime background that some aspects of the 1987 Defence White Paper need to be judged, for though we are currently not threatened, we are probably more exposed in a defence sense that we have been since 1942.

There is much in the White Paper with which most thinking people would agree. There is clearly need for such supportive measures as effective reserves, survelliance, efficient and comprehensive defence industry, intelligence, command and control, communications, research, some bases in the north, integration of the Reserve and Permanent Armies, easier call out of Reserves, and many others. While some points may be arguable, overall there is much support for the general thrust of these clear needs.

It is in the field of strategy, with its major consequential international and military effects, that there is much room for contention.

The starting point perhaps lies in definitions.

It is not entirely clear why definitions of Australia's areas of "primary strategic interest" and of "direct military interest" should be so closely delineated in such a public document, unless it is to limit in the public and international mind the perception of Australia's interests—or perhaps to tailor our interests to what it is thought could be achieved within current allotted resources.

Be that as it may, the definitions of our own area of primary strategic interest as "covering South-East Asia, the Eastern Indian Ocean. and the South-West Pacific" seems strangely limiting.

The major local Asian powers, and maritime powers at that—Japan, China, and India—are excluded from such a definition, and from such an exclusion flow many deductions on the capability of nations "in our region".

But such a definition seems to ignore geographical and practical reality, for the mainlands of all three of these nations are closer to the mainland of Australia than are parts of South East Asia, such as Burma. Indeed, the island bases of all three (Okinawa, Hainan and the Andaman Islands) are closer to mainland Australia than not only Burma, but much of Thailand and Vietnam.

Can it be argued seriously that major changes in attitudes or alignments of such nations as Kampuchea, Thailand, Burma, or even Vietnam are more important strategically to Australia than changes in attitudes or alignments involving the major local powers of China, Japan and Indian—nations which are not only the centres of the greatest regional populations, industrial output, military power and maritime capability, but also of the greatest trading interest to Australia?

Perhaps it is a legacy of the old SEATO days, and the term "South-East Asia" has become too historic and ingrained a geographical description in our jargon. The reality of South-East Asia is that of a number of disparate nations each being of fundamentally different levels of importance to our security.

It can be argued that events in the few months since the release of the White Paper have already cast doubts on the adequacy and relevance of the definitions given, for the first major event possibly affecting our defence forces concerned Fiji—a geographical locality on the very boundary of our regions of prime strategic or military interest, as defined. The second was the announced intention to despatch R.A.N. divers to the Persian Gulf—a geographical locality far beyond our defined area of "prime strategic" or "direct military" interest.

The reality, of course, is that our trade routes to nations bordering the Gulf are of considerable importance to Australia—for much of our imported black oil is sourced there, and we have valuable export trade in such commodities as live sheep and foodstuffs of various kinds.

We have an abiding interest in the security of such sea lands, of those passing through the South West and South Pacific, and of Australian ships using them, distant though they may be. And ANZUS is a two-way treaty.

So much for definitions, but they can mislead and delude with such statements as "and in South East Asia, Australia's power projection capabilities especially for strike and interdiction, are considerable by regional standards".

Of course, if one has removed India and China from the definition of "regional" maybe that is so, but those nations are much closer, more militarily capable, and more relevant to South East Asia than are we.

The White Paper has moved somewhat from the largely defensive continental-type strategy espoused in the Dibb Report, to one claiming to be based on the concept of defence in depth.

To a degree this claim is true, but, although they are in our defined "area of direct military interest", there is little mention of obtaining real defence in depth by adjusting our capabilities to be able to assist our friends and allies in the archipelago across our northern and north-eastern approaches. Such a policy, even if it failed, would buy time for our own defence, as in World War II, and give us much greater defence in depth.

This logical requirement, for there would be much internal and external political and military pressure to take advantage of such possibilities in time of serious threat, would require further development of skills in island warfare techniques (often without airfields), in amphibious operations, and in jungle warfare. These requirements seem to be missing in the White Paper, even though some of them would be required for the defence of our own island territories. The recent events in the South West Pacific seem to reinforce this view, as does the slightly firmer defence agreement with Papua New Guinea.

Additionally, while supporting the U.S. concept of deterrence, and indeed, for our own defence, canvassing to a limited degree that "prospective advantages both as a means of deterring attack, or if that fails deterring escalation, reinforce the need for capabilities providing the option for a retaliatory response", the paper does not develop this possible strategy further.

There are many strategists who would argue that a strategy of deterrence holds out great advantages in terms of cost and resources for a technically-advanced medium power of small population, such as Australia.

In our case, conventional deterrence to any power outside the range of Australian-based aircraft could well be provided by a strong submarine force, including a nuclear-powered element. A mire six conventional boats, however advanced in current technology, can provide only a very modest deterrent when compared with such a force strongly supported by two or three nuclears. Indeed a number of naval powers strongly favour mixed conventional and nuclear powered submarine forces as a most cost effective mix.

Evidence of the flexibility and effectiveness of nuclear-powered submarines was demonstrated convincingly during the Falklands War when the nuclear-powered H.M.S. *Conqueror* was despatched in secret at high underwater speed and subsequently intercepted, tracked and sank the Argentinean cruiser *General Belgrano.* After this event the Argentine Navy withdrew from the general area and was subsequently unable to support the Argentine Army ashore on the Falkland Islands.

To deter any attack on our shipping or raids on our territory by our possession of an evident capability to retaliate in kind while at the same time being able to provide some capability to defend our shipping, offshore territories and installations, and deal with minor raids would seem to be a cost-effective defence policy for Australia.

Such a policy would seem, in defence and international terms, to be more effective than one of merely awaiting an attack somewhere in our huge "sea-air" gap and attempting then to deal with it, without retaliation.

Of course, there will be those who may argue that Australia's possession of nuclear-powered submarines might be seen as being provocative. Perhaps some may choose to see it this way, but until recent years Australia has always had a strong navy including long range strike units, and since at least 7 nations operate nuclear power submarines in the Indian and Pacific Oceans from time to time, our possession of such vessels could hardly be considered rationally in such a light.

The White Paper seems on solid ground when it asserts that "By its very nature, the defence of Australia and its territories emphasises maritime warfare capabilities. The Australian Defence Force must be able to conduct maritime operations to prevent an adversary from substantial use or exploitation of our maritime approaches". However, this overall philosophy does not seem to be followed fully in subsequent policy development.

In some maritime areas, the White Paper is realistic and down to earth, for example in the need for a two-ocean navy, land based maritime air operations, including the RAAF inflight refuelling, a mine countermeasures force, the need for some facilities to move to Jervis Bay—the new command arrangements, and the need to defend our bases (though it makes little provision for the ground and air defence of the important Cockburn Sound).

In others it is less realistic.

The assertion that the entry into force of the Treaty of Rarotonga instituting the South Pacific Nuclear Free Zone is a gain for Australian and regional security, and that the Treaty also protects Western strategic interests in the region seems arguable. It doesn't lie easily with proclaiming that we are an aligned nation, the paper's strong support of ANZUS, and the defence arrangements with the United States.

The main arm of American power relevant to our region is the U.S. Navy which is heavily reliant on nuclear propulsion and, in part, weapons. One would have thought that any constraints on U.S. Naval operations could act against our, and Western, overall security interests.

The paper states that the threat to Australia from submarines is low. Though, given our friendly relations with other countries, this may be true at present, the assertion seems strange from a number of viewpoints.

Firstly, there are six Indian Ocean and western Pacific Ocean nations which are not in the western alliance but which have the capability, if they so wished, to operate submarines off our coasts.

Secondly, the submarine seems to be the only weapon system that has been singled out for such a definitive statement. There would appear, for instance, to much more chance of such a threat developing than that of a serious air threat to Australia, for only one nation (USSR, from Vietnam) would seem to have aircraft of a suitable type to reach (with in-flight refuelling) our more southerly areas.

Thirdly, interdiction of the seaborne trade of an island trading nation is always an attractive military strategy. Such action formed the main move directly against Australia in both World War I (by Germany) and World War II (by Germany and Japan). Given that a growing number of nations now have submarines, their possible future use against Australia seems to warrant higher priority to Anti-Submarine Warfare than has been accorded.

Another area of major concern is what many believe to be a mistaken appreciation of the possible future threat to, and the importance of Australian trade. It should here be noted that, despite the increase in size and load capacity of aircraft, shipping still carries no less than 96% of our imports and exports. The White Paper states that:

> Australia's overseas trade routes are diverse and their comprehensive interdiction would be credible only in the unlikely circumstances of protracted global conflict. Under those conditions, threats to international shipping would affect many countries. Countries which have important interests in the free flow of trade would seek to protect international shipping. Australia would then contribute to wider efforts to protect international trade, operating in our own area in accordance with the procedures of the Radford-Collins Agreement.

This is a comforting statement, but does it bear up to examination?

Firstly, it must be said that "comprehensive interdiction" would not be necessary to cause grave disruption to our economy. For example, the loss of only a few ships carrying oil to our refineries, iron ore to our steel works or bauxite-alumina to our aluminium refineries would cause great dislocation to those most important industries. The loss of only a few ships bringing urgently needed supplies for our Defence Force and Defence Industry could cripple our defence effort. Any nation possessing a submarine force of only modest size could pose us a most serious problem as could the use of mines, surface raiders, or, in some areas, aircraft.

Secondly, the merchant fleets of our allies have dwindled greatly in recent years and there is no guarantee that international shipping would continue to be available in sufficient quantity to ensure our exports and imports. Unlike the Persian Gulf scene, we are not an essential source of world supplies, for most of our commodities can be obtained in quantity from other areas.

If the probable loss of ships, and insurance rates, became high, shipping availability may reduce. Additionally, attacks on Australian shipping may well occur at the same time as there are hostilities in other areas, and shipping may be withdrawn for priority tasks elsewhere.

Thirdly, though Britain moved earlier in the Gulf War, it took some years before the U.S. undertook protection of its own shipping. There can be no surety, though we may so hope, that under all circumstances in any limited war involving Australia, other countries would seek to protect international shipping in what would be to them the remote area around us.

We would have to protect shipping ourselves, for we would be the nation with most to lose.

There is a comfortable statement that "We are a net exporter of energy". But one must look carefully at this statement. It is, of course, true for coal, natural gas, and some oil products, but our road transport, aircraft and most trains and ships run on oil or its products. We are already down to supplying only 60% of our needs. This percentage is falling, and we produce no black oil needed for lubricants. Without guaranteed oil supplies, the nation would grind to a halt, and oil in quantity can only reach most of our great cities by sea. Maybe the recent discoveries in the Timor Sea will prove up as considerable oil reserves, but their location will make them highly vulnerable in war involving us and there can be no surety of supplies from the North West Shelf in such a situation. We would have to insure that tankers from overseas reached our ports—and for this we will need not only strong naval escort forces but more Australian-manned tankers.

The White Paper goes on to state:

> Most of the essential needs of the civil community could be met without external supply if appropriate measures of conservation and rationing were introduced. Those essential items that are imported (including defence equipment and spare parts, industrial machinery, transport equipment, lubricants and rubber) could be stockpiled or alternative sources arranged—even if at higher cost—if there is any change in our current judgement about the remote prospect of global conflict.

As the Master Mariners comment in a recent paper, expressing their concern at the current inability of the R.A.N. to protect Australian shipping adequately:

> It must be carrying optimism to extreme lengths to believe that the advent of any threat of hostilities would give Australia sufficient time to contract for the delivery of those things enumerated in the above statement, pay for them, and have them delivered to Australian ports in sufficient quantities for any predetermined time scale of hostilities, as well as obtaining the many items of war material and armaments that the armed forces may require from overseas![1]

One can hardly imagine any Government moving to build such stockpiles short of a direct threat to this country.

The White Paper includes further statements endeavouring to portray the risk to our merchant shipping in a rosier light than many maritime authorities believe is justified:

> Effective interdiction of our trade in open ocean areas would require wide area surveillance capabilities such as satellites or over-the-horizon radar with

> real-time communications links to attacking forces. No regional country has now such capabilities and their development is not in prospect. Surveillance and intelligence information of this kind is unlikely to be made available to a regional adversary.

This again is a surprising statement. Maybe again it is delusion by the definition of "regional". However, there are now a number of nations with satellite design and launching capability and there can be no surety that, in any war involving us, satellite and other intelligence will not be passed by a third party to our adversaries, should they not possess such capability themselves. Indeed, even were this not to be so, modern submarines—even conventional ones—have very long ears and a greater intercept capability than in the past.

In both world wars, German surface raiders, sometimes using their seaplanes, were able to intercept many ships far out on the seas particularly off our West Coast—and far from "focal areas" where the raiders themselves could more easily have been detected and sunk.

One wonders whether some authors of the White Paper have studied our own maritime history in sufficient depth, for Australia is very vulnerable to attack on its seaborne trade. Modern inventions such as satellites, sea-borne helicopters and readily fitted stand-off missiles seem to make it more so whether from submarines, surface raiders or from aircraft.

Indeed it would seem that attacks on Australian shipping might be a very attractive form of pressure for an attacker in any level of warfare at far below the "global" level, with maybe less international implications and certainly requiring less resources and involving less international implications and certainly requiring less resources and involving less military and political problems than would raids on our northern coast.

The Navy and Merchant Navy steeped in the realities and with great experience of maritime warfare, of course, know this, but in the form of defence organisation Australia has developed, their voices seem lost and unheeded in a plethora of committees.

At a recent seminar in Sydney, the Secretary of the Seamen's Union called for the Royal Australian Navy to defend Australian merchant ships in the Persian Gulf. The Master Mariners are themselves most concerned at the lack of naval capability to defend merchant shipping. This has led them to take the unprecedented step of voicing publicly their unease.

The White Paper omits consideration of such matters, but the implications seem clear enough. Unless provided with a reasonable level of protection our ships may not sail when needed.

The need to defend shipping carrying essential imports and some exports, perhaps to considerable distances from our shores, taken with the advantages of being able to influence and assist our friends and allies in the archipelagic regions off our shores point strongly not only to a considerable increase in our escort strength but to the need for air-power at sea with the fleet. There will be many occasions when air support cannot be given from shore bases in Australia, not only through questions of distance and time, but also as fighter aircraft in particular may be required for priority defence of shore bases and cities.

There needs to be a re-examination of the "carrier" question noting that, as the British have shown, it may be possible to greatly reduce costs while obtaining a reasonable level of air capability by converting merchant ship hulls for the carriage of VSTOL (Jump Jets) and helicopters. Such vessels have the added important advantage of being able to carry a battalion of troops and much of their light equipment, this adding greatly to the mobility of the Defence Force.

Ships at sea are now vulnerable to missiles fired at long range whether by submarines, surface ship or aircraft. Such attacks are best dealt with by destroying or neutralising the launching platform and not by trying to combat the missile with last ditch defence. For this, airpower with the fleet is essential.

Regarding personnel, the White Paper, acknowledges that "our people—the men and women of our fighting forces and our defence civilian staff—are our most valuable asset and a vital resource in the security of Australia".

It acknowledges the need to attract, train and retain skilled personnel, and that to be successful in attracting sufficient people of the right calibre, the Government must offer rewarding and challenging careers, and competitive pay, allowances, and conditions of service.

One wonders, however, whether all these aspects are being

addressed in line with the above emphasis. The increased drain from the services, particularly of officers and senior NCOs, leads one to believe that they are not.

Conditions of service in many areas have not kept pace with those available in other professions which do not entail the same risks and family separation as in the armed forces. Technology in some areas in the Defence Force has fallen behind and does not present the necessary incentive or challenge for keen young, technical minds. Platforms, weapons and equipment at the cutting edge in a number of areas compare unfavourably with those of equivalent services of other nations. The small carrots of exchange service with the British and American forces have been cut back to the detriment of standards of expertise, professional knowledge and experience.

Unless some means of providing a leavening of overseas service is found, repeated postings to the remote, hot, and arid north of our country, where jobs for wives and education for children may be scarce, is hardly likely to prove either financially attractive, professionally rewarding, or personally satisfying to ambitious and talented personnel.

Likewise too many postings to the many stultifying jobs in the huge defence complexes in Canberra and too few to the ships, aircraft squadrons, and battalions, which keen young men aspire to command, deaden interest and military expertise and, finally, a desire to serve on.

And what of the resources needed for adequate defence? In this the White Paper states:

> There is a need for realism in expectations of the resources that governments will be able to allocate to Defence. If we are to achieve the levels of defence capability and the priorities reflected in this Paper, there is need, over the life of the programme, for an allocation of resources generally within the order of 2.6 percent to 3.0 percent of G.D.P. Annual allocation to Defence will of course continue to be subject to the normal reviews of our economic circumstances and other policy imperatives, as well as changes in our strategic outlook.

While, indeed, this has been the general situation for some

years, and of course there is a need for realism, the time seems to have arrived when some aspects of such statements need questioning.

It would seem that we may no longer, if we are wise, be in the situation whereby it is a question of what Governments may *be able to* allocate but rather what circumstances dictate they *should* allocate to Defence if our succeeding generations are to have a reasonable chance of adequate national security. After all, many countries—including our main allies, the U.S. and Britain—expend a much greater percentage of G.N.P. on defence than we do. Can we reasonably any longer expect the U.S. to underwrite our defence while we do not pay our way?

Additionally, to enable the building of an effective defence force, many perceive a need for the nation to move away from the inevitable "stop-go" policies implicit in yearly reviews, subject to all sorts of political currents. There seems a need for steady and largely bipartisan policies with adequate ongoing financial allocations to support five year programmes. Small fluctuations there can be, but not to the extent that they effect the confidence and efficiency of the Defence Force and Defence Industry.

Of course, there will be cries that increased expenditure would adversely affect our economy. This, however, is not necessarily so, for if great effort is made (and this seems to be happening) to produce a major percentage of capital equipment in Australia, this would result (as it has in some other countries) in a huge stimulus to industry, research and development, and employment. Indeed, much would flow back into the national coffers by all sorts of taxation returns.

With understanding policies and efficient production, we could become (as the Pacific patrol boat is demonstrating) a ready source of defence equipment support for the nations of the South Pacific, to the benefit of all nations involved. We might even find that the requirements of Social Security, now astonishingly about equivalent in the Federal Budget to the addition of the total of expenditures on Health, Education and Defence, would reduce as industry picked up and unemployment dropped further.

In other words some re-allocation gradually within the budget need not necessarily result in a diminution of Social Services for those who really need it.

Additionally, a really close examination and pruning of the huge staffs, both civilian and military, in Canberra and in the various headquarters, would not only throw up resources for us in the teeth arms, but result in greater job satisfaction for many personnel. Happily, this process may well be starting, in line with the general move in industry towards lean and hungry head-office staffs with a maximum delegation of responsibility elsewhere.

From this examination of the 1987 Defence White Paper, what overall changes now seem to be warranted?

Firstly, there needs to be consideration whether the definitions of our "areas of primary strategic interest" and " area of direct military interest" are in need of revision, or indeed needed at all. We must take into account the changing maritime, long range deployment, and strike capabilities of the various great nations of Asia, and the effect this may have on the balance of power and future stability.

Secondly, the proposed strategy needs re-consideration with a thorough examination of the possibilities of a strategy based primarily on greater defence in depth, and a strong element of deterrence. The acquisition not only of aerial tankers for inflight refuelling of strike aircraft, but also of a small force of nuclear-powered submarines to supplement the new conventional boats seems highly desirable, for training as well as for deterrence.

Thirdly, the need to protect not only our coastal shipping but essential imports and exports, perhaps out to considerable distances from the continent, must be incorporated firmly in our defence policy. Means of providing the Navy with air-power at sea with the fleet must be re-examined. It could be that the British example of the cheap conversion of merchant ships able not only of limited support for the Navy but of lifting and supporting a battalion of troops and airforce equipment might be a most cost-effective solution.

Fourthly, the requirement to implement the defence in depth principle, including an evident capability to go to the aid of friendly island nations in our area, must be translated into increased emphasis on amphibious, jungle, and island warfare capabilities together with means of transport and support of the Australian Defence Force by sea as by air.

Fifthly, great attention needs to be paid to ensuring that life in the Australian Defence Force offers rewarding and challenging careers, filled with interest and excitement, and competitive pay, allowances and conditions of service.

And lastly, without resolve by successive Governments to stand by their pronouncements and programmes on defence by providing the necessary finance over many years, any White Paper on our Defence will be largely meaningless.

In conclusion, it must be said that the 1987 Defence White Paper represents a significant step forward in addressing the nation's defence problem. However, its proposed strategy needs closer review.

For an island nation like Australia, with a small but technically advanced population, there seems a strong argument to improve the deterrent element of our Defence Force; and perhaps the White Paper needs to be a trifle—bluer.

NOTE

1. **Pacific Defence Reporter,** December/January 1988, p.204.

Comments

Frank Broeze

Although these comments are in first instance intended as a response to Admiral Robertson's paper, I should also like to take this opportunity to make some general points and to indicate some areas of concern which, I think, may be shared by many. As Admiral Robertson's paper has already suggested, it is not possible to consider 'technical' points of defence planning and procurement without reference to the much broader issues of Australia's place in the world; my view is that these broader issues cannot be raised often and emphatically enough. They refer to the policies and purpose of Australia as well as to the policy makers' perception of the world within which defence policies and strategies have to be developed.

First, I can only wholeheartedly agree with Admiral Robertson that there can be no more doubt about the fact that the Indian Ocean region is of primary strategic importance to Australia. Our country's trade with many littoral states as well as across the ocean; political events and instability in the region—punctuated with major outbreaks of violence such as the Gulf War; the involvement of the superpowers, of whom the United States is linked to Australia through an alliance; the continued commitment of Australia to the Five Power Defence Arrangement, which includes Singapore as well as Malaysia; the growth of national defence capabilities and many other issues make it imperative for the Australian Government and the Department of Defence to fully incorporate the region in their strategic and political calculations. This does, of course, not mean that the importance attached to other regions in Australia's wider geographical environment, such as Northeast Asia or the Southwest Pacific, should be diminished, but rather that one more vital ingredient is added to all those which collectively determine the direction of our national security policy. Moreover, in view of the geographical reality that many of the northern approaches of Australia pass through or skirt the eastern longitudes of the Indian Ocean region, it could be said that the major strategic orientation of the country has firmly switched towards the West-to-North segment of the compass.

As Minister Beazley in his paper and as the 1987 White Paper on Defence have indicated, this reorientation has begun. Major initiatives have been taken, such as the transfer of a major part of the Royal Australian Navy from Sydney to Cockburn Sound, the construction of the Tindal airbase in the Northern Territory, and the building of another airbase at Derby. Within the naval component of defence new building programmes of submarines, frigates and patrol boats are designed to further enhance Australian defence capabilities in the Indian Ocean region. However, to suggest, as Minister Beazley emphatically does in the title of his address, that these initiatives add up to giving Australia a "Two Ocean Navy", that is a capacity to project adequate naval power into both Indian and Pacific Oceans at the same time, is to be more than optimistic. Not just for stylistic reasons, the text of the Minister's address refers repeatedly to a

Navy "located on two shorelines", which is a much more realistic description of Australia's maritime posture. Admiral Robertson has been very firm in his criticism of the Minister on this point and in this I can only agree with him. It is most doubtful indeed, whether Australia will have the capability to operate effectively in both areas, or even one, in case of real emergency.

If there is no doubt about the strategic importance of the Indian Ocean region and about the fact that Australia needs to be able to project force into the area, disagreement immediately starts, when one asks what force, where, and why? Admiral Robertson has raised very pertinent questions about the total context, within which we have to consider the build-up and use (or potential use) of naval force, when he demanded a broader geographical definition of Australia's areas of "primary strategic interest" and of "direct military interest". The concepts provided by the Department of Defence in its White Paper, limited to the eastern Indian Ocean (without any further clarification), Southeast Asia and the Southwest Pacific are patently too narrow for any realistic scenario, as they exclude all major powers whose policies in future years will determine developments in the region: Japan, China and India. Suggestions, as yet no more than kites in the wind, of a tripartite alliance between Australia, Japan and the United States, despite their apparent unworldiness indicate more clearly the direction of things to come than a myopic staring at Australia's immediate environment.

More importantly, whatever one's perception of the appropriate theatre for the development and display of Australia's naval forces, there appears to be very little thought in the Department of Defence being given to the effective coordination of national policy and strategic doctrine. Henry Kissinger, a political scientist who became one of the keenest practitioners of his own art, insisted that any defence policy be tested against the following three elemental questions: What is the national interest?, what is the national purpose?, and how can these goals be most effectively reached? Obviously, it is a lot easier to put than to answer these questions! The quip is that in the United States alone some 40,000 political scientists are engaged in defining just what the American national interest is. Nevertheless, it is clear that, in order to shape Australia's national military/naval policies and strategies there must be some concrete perceptions of her medium- and long-term objectives as well as a concerted attempt to match resources, through weapon system and manpower strategies, with those objectives. As Admiral Robertson has emphasised, there is only eloquent silence or rather meaningless generalities, when it comes to the White Paper's discussion of this fundamental context for future defence planning; but, similarly, Minister Beazley's address is in this regard disappointingly myopic and narrow.

Specifically, there is no mention whatsoever of the Indian Ocean region (in fact, the "eastern Indian Ocean" has been deleted from the list of "those regions that are of primary strategic concern to us"), despite the fact that the expansion of the Indian Navy is given a place of importance in the Minister's statement. As Admiral Robertson has stressed, a successful foreign policy must be underwritten by a commensurate and credible defence stance, although it is, of course, true that it is not only the defence posture of a country which determines its security and the significance of its role in international politics. As Australia, however, because of the particular nature of her economy has little influence in the international arena (and, in fact, as a result of her economic policies has a tendency to alienate rather than befriend many countries in her region) and also cannot derive much strength from her ideological stance, a close coordination between defence and foreign policies seems more than normally called for. It certainly requires the adoption of a wider geographical perspective in shaping the theatre for which Australian defence is planned and on which its forces are to be deployed or, at least, are to be capable to be deployed; or, on the other hand, if it is clear that force cannot be deployed for a certain purpose at greater distance, it is best to be clear about that.

To suggest that there is a connection between either the concept of the defence of Australia's overseas trade or the active implementation of the military clauses of ANZUS and the decision to send twenty Australian divers to the Gulf for mine hunting purposes, is to overlook the essential nature of the political context, within which the divers are to be used. Their mission is, above all, an exercise in the demonstration of western solidarity in the face of regional Indian Ocean instability—neither of the two of which figure on the Department of Defence's list of strategic priorities. Similarly, it is impossible to find any reference to consideration being given to underwriting Australian interests and policies in Northeast Asia through fleet visits or other naval signals.

In short, Australian defence planning and policy appears to have a far too narrow geographical and political base. At no stage the fundamental question is put as to what constitutes the country's national purpose: what mixture is it, to summarize the opposing poles of the spectrum as briefly as possible, of "peace through security" and "security through peace"? In other words, should defence policies, and hence material procurement, only be based on wartime or at least "violent"scenarios, or shouldn't they also, or perhaps even predominantly, be geared towards providing a supportive role for policy initiatives which, in turn, could alleviate the need to actually use force? It is, under present-day circumstances, amazing how often, and in how many different forums, the writings of Admiral Alfred Thayer Mahan are still regarded as the ultimate wisdom on the application of seapower; much more useful, I would suggest, is the slender but highly thoughtful **The Political Uses of Sea Power** by Edward N. Luttwak.[1] It is little more than stating the obvious that since 1945 seapower has had a far more important political than military role to play, even if, as in the Cuban missile crisis, there could be acute confrontation between the superpowers. But especially for minor powers, such as Australia, who cannot be expected to be easily involved in a hot war yet live in a volatile and politically very dynamic world, reflecting on the peacetime role of maritime power seems an absolutely vital ingredient in the formulation of defence strategy and procurement.

It is true in the Defence White Paper repeated mention is made of the stability of Southeast Asia as an important national objective, and Minister Beazley in his statement has stressed the increased operational capacity of submarines and surface vessels based at H.M.S. Stirling, but it is not at all clear in what ways the two are related. Submarines, in particular, are hardly suitable for underwriting diplomacy.

In practice, there are, inevitably, major obstacles in coordinating the efforts of the Departments of Foreign Affairs and Defence, even if both ministers involved and Cabinet as a whole were committed to such coordination; very little evidence, however, of the presence of such a commitment exists. Pragmatic and bureaucratic struggles over budget distribution seem to take precedence. It is, therefore, very much the task and responsibility of such independent forums as ours here, to continue to insist on the raising of these fundamental issues. It should, however, be well understood, even if such a meeting of department minds could be achieved, major questions and dilemmas remain. One of the most significant of these must, necessarily, be that of the relation between the force best suited for peacetime use and that calculated to carry optimal weight and power in wartime: the two may well be quite different in strength and character, so that creative compromises are indispensable. It is on this score that I have some major concerns about the thrust of Admiral Robertson's paper.

First, as in both the Defence White Paper he so roundly criticises and Minister Beazley's statement, he adopts an almost exclusively wartime scenario for the development of his thoughts on the composition and deployment of the force which, in his mind, would constitute a Royal Australian Navy adequate for the national purpose. There is no indication of the diplomatic role of the fleet, nor does he accept the necessity to consider the political implications of the adoption of particular weapon systems, such as nuclear-driven submarines. Here I do not mean domestic political considerations, as the debate over nuclear-powered submarines quite properly needs to be fought out in the public domain, but the international repercussions of such a major shift in technology and capability.

Moreover, the questions of finances and resources can never be overlooked; Admiral Robertson, and here I fully agree with him, cannot find the present level of funding of the Department of Defence satisfactory nor the manner in which the actual budget is being spent, but to argue, as he does, for both seaborne airpower and nuclear-powered submarines without taking into account the inevitable consequences for the remainder of the R.A.N. and the overall Defence budget can hardly be called realistic.

A fundamental element of naval planning and strategy is, therefore, to consider just what mix of weapon systems represents the optimal compromise for both current peacetime and potential wartime/violent use. As the tactical efficacy of each system depends very much on the political/military environment (including the military needs and strengths of all powers who enter into the strategic equation) within which Australian interests are pursued as well as its own intrinsic tactical capabilities, there is an important technological dimesion to the problem of how to achieve that compromise: if, for example, it is decided that air cover is needed over a certain distance away from

Australia's northwest coast, the question becomes one of which weapon system can most adequately (in terms of both mission capability and cost effectiveness) produce the desired result. But if, as the Defence White Paper emphasizes, one of the major missions of Australian defence policy is "the continued stability of our region", then it will be much more difficult to decide whether the total number of frigates should be six or eight, the number of submarines to be stationed at H.M.S. Stirling, similarly, three or four, or indeed, whether the proposed mix between submarine forces and ASW capacity is the most appropriate one.

To my mind, the adoption of wartime scenarios, based on the concept of a fortress Australia, as determinants of the composition of the fleet is highly dubious as a means towards that goal of regional stability.

It is very doubtful, whether submarines are useful tools for effective diplomacy; it is even more improbable that the adoption of nuclear propulsion by Australia (quite apart from the damage it would do to other sectors of the defence effort) would be a positive factor. However that may be, and however difficult it may be to find the optional material mix for a peacetime Australian navy, it is remarkable that neither in the White Paper and the Minister's address nor in Admiral Robertson's paper projections are given as to the current and prospective strength and composition of the navies of the other powers in Australia's wider region (except for the references to the acquisition by India of one nuclear-powered submarine). This is not to suggest that, as in the times of Britain's uncontested hegemony when a simple counting of battleships sufficed to establish an international league table of naval powers, naval procurement should be based on some mathematical formula relating to other navies in the region; on the contrary, such a policy would be both foolish and counterproductive, but it should never be lost sight of that naval power is not absolute but relative, and that its efficacy depends on the environment in which it has to operate (and also here, I must stress, both peacetime and wartime conditions should be considered).

Obviously, one should not be alarmed, let alone become an alarmist, because India in recent years has significantly expanded her maritime power. There is no reason why Australia should automatically respond in any specific way. But as the expansion of the Indian navy causes, wittingly or unwittingly, reverberations through the region, it is the task of defence planners and their advisers to take careful stock of the impact made by such developments, in terms of the interests and political/military stance of both the countries in the region and the superpowers. It seems far-fetched to suggest that the unhappy events in Fiji might lead to any wish on the part of the Indian government to intervene in a manner comparable to that used in Sri Lanka. But there is no doubt that the expansion of India's regional power will, at some stage, be of interest to Indonesia, our immediate northern neighbour and the strongest of the states of Southeast Asia whose stability is one of Australia's main concerns, or the United States, our ally in ANZUS. In consequence, at that stage, Australia's interest also will be involved. The implications of such a situation can, of course, now not be overseen, but within the scope of present-day defence policy making and naval strategy planning there seems to be little or no opportunity for Australia to respond through, for example, naval visits to Indian ports. Indeed, one of the most disturbing aspects of the "pure wartime scenario" formation of naval policy is its great lack of political sophistication and flexibility.

Two other issues which immediately come to mind of comparable or even more significant issues of this kind are the total lack of any discussion about the actual purpose of the Australia-New Zealand defence alliance, and the general tensions and contradictions inherent in Australia's simultaneously adhering to its alliance relationship with the United States (of which the exact nature is clear to no one) and following a policy of self reliance and independent initiative.

It would be grossly unfair to assign the major blame for this situation to Minister Beazley, or even the Department of Defence and its at times caustic but like-minded critics like Admiral Robertson. It is a fact of Australian political life that defence is not a vote winner. No doubt most observers would agree with me that with the present Minister the Department of Defence has a more purposeful and determined leader than it has had for many years. But even so, whether for electoral reasons or otherwise, defence needs can still only be explained and justified in simplistic terms or general statements of intent which bear far too little relevance to the complex world around us. It is, therefore, also doubtful, whether one can expect a Defence White Paper, or a thorough review of existing policies more than once every twelve years or so. It must be feared, too, that in between successive White Papers preciously little flexibility in terms of a willingness and capability to respond to political and military change in the region will exist.

Finally, I should like to make two general points. First, with regard to the future composition of the R.A.N., I totally disagree with Admiral Robertson on the point of nuclear-powered submarines. Whatever the reasons of other countries to go in for mixed under-water fleets, Australia does not have the need, political will or resources to take such a step. Naval aviation, on the other hand, I think is a must for serious reconsideration, partly for the obvious increase in naval, surveillance and overall military capacity which it represents, but also for the increase in political influence which emanates from its greater political visibility and mobility in regional deployment.

Neither the present nor the future submarine force of the R.A.N. (when it will be ready) is suitable for "showing the flag" purposes, and its destroyers, frigates and patrol boats do not consitute very impressive hardware. A review of the fleet's composition is highly desirable. At the moment it is not, as optimistically asserted, a "Two Ocean Navy"; at the most, it is a "One Ocean Navy" split in two parts and located on two of Australia's shores. If the strategic importance of the Indian Ocean is to be taken seriously, much more maritime capability will need to be based in Australia's western and northern parts.

Secondly, such a full reappraisal cannot go without a thorough analysis of the entire structure of the Department of Defence and, in particular, its manpower policy. Not only is there far too much federalism and rivalry in the relationship between the three main arms, but the department's topheavy bureaucracy and its still highly unsatisfactory employment conditions for active naval personnel make it virtually impossible to embark on major procurement initiatives. Again, however unsatisfactory the present situatiion may be, it is to the credit of Minister Beazley that he has achieved that much. But if nothing changes, one must fear that the very commitments to new weapon systems will go so much at the expense of the serving personnel and funds for exercises, etc. that we shall largely have a collection of uninhabited hulls.

It is absolutely imperative to undertake such a total review, if

Australia is to acquire anything which might properly be called a "Two Ocean Navy".

NOTE

1. **The Political Uses of Sea Power** (Baltimore: Johns Hopkins University Press, 1974).

Comments

P.G.N.Kennedy

I wish to make a comment on Rear Admiral Robertson's advocacy of Australia requiring nuclear submarines.Perhaps though I should first explain that until last July (1987) I was Chief of Naval Operational Requirements, Policy and Plans—the "desk" responsible for formulating the Navy's major and minor capital equipment (fighting) requirements. It is time to say that none of the Admirals of the navy nor any of its senior serving submarine officers (policy or operational) thought that the navy should acquire nuclear submarines at this stage. I think it would be equally true to say that all of us confidently expect that the following generation will be nuclear. The reasons for this are:

- First, that at present Australia has no nuclear engineering infrastructure or industry capable of supporting nuclear submarines—the solutions were either one of prohibitive expense or reliance on some third party such as the US navy thousands of miles away in Pearl Harbor. Neither solution was thought feasible.
- That whilst the nuclear submarine has much greater mobility in getting to and from an assigned station (and therefore theoretically one would need fewer for a given level of "on station" presence) the nuclear submarine is very much more expensive. Economics favoured the conventional.
- The type of nuclear vessel Australia might just conceivably

have been able to afford (at the expense of other programme requirements) such as the small French Rubis-Class could not have accommodated all the suite of sensors and other elements of the overall fire-control that we wanted, i.e. the nuclear propulsion system of a smallish submarine such as the Rubis requires a disproportionally larger percentage of the hull volume—it would therefore be less suitable in its fighting capabilities.

- Much of the sea area to the north of Australia, particularly in its archipelagic region, is shallow water where the larger nuclear submarine is less suitable for many purposes than the smaller conventional submarine.
- Finally—public opinion. Seemingly much of the public fails to discriminate between "nuclear propelled" and "nuclear armed". Use of the word nuclear quite often invokes immediate hysteria. Although it is ultimately for the politicians to make that sort of decision, I don't think any of us thought the community at large is well enough versed or prepared to accept that Australia should now acquire a nuclear submarine—although some well informed people like Admiral Robertson obviously are.

Comments

Robert H. Bruce

I want to raise a few questions about the policy enunciated by the Minister of Defence in Chapter 1 and in the Defence White Paper. My questions concern the adequacy of the evidence on which the premises are based and of the policy inferences drawn from the premises, and the incompleteness of the analysis in regard to insufficient attention given to implications of the policy and inadequate integration of the policy with Australia's overall security needs, goals, and actions.

First, questions can be raised about the adequacy of the

premises on which the policy is based. Admiral Robertson and Frank Broeze, for example, challenge one of the major premises of the policy when they declare that the area designated to be the area of Australia's strategic interest is too limited. How far from Australia should the area of strategic interest extend? And will Australia, with its limited military capabilities, be able to do much about what happens within that area? How far out from Australia is it that Australia needs to develop forces that can meet threats? These are among the important questions that need further investigation and discussion.

There are questions also about the adequacy of assumptions about future technological developments. There is constant, unrelenting development of new technologies with military implications and diffusion of new military technology to the Indian Ocean area. Australia, like other states, is confronted with assessing these developments and basing policy on those assessments. "Each political actor", Barry Buzan has observed, "faces a central security worry, not only about the quantity and quality of military technology in the hands of other actors, but also about the pace and direction of change in these variables."[1] Are assessments about technological changes and their likely effects that underpin the policy adequate?

There are also questions about another premise on which the policy rests: the security relationship with the United States. This security relationship is a foundation stone for the policy. The policy assumes a future commitment of the United States to resupply equipment in the event of a war involving Australia. Is this a safe assumption on which to build a policy? Relations between states within an alliance change; existing alliances evolve. The Australian-American security relationship is no exception. It can be useful to view the alliance as one example of the general phenomenon of alliances in international relations. In alliances, Robert Jervis has noted, some leaders "have a tendency to overestimate the degree of common interest involved".[2] And, interests change. "Whereas national values are permanent and unchanging, unaffected by changes in historical circumstances, interests are context dependent; they can and do change," Alexander George has observed.[3] For the United States, Australia is an interest that can help it to protect its own values. But there is nothing permanent, unchanging about America's need for Australia. "'Interests,'" George has observed, "are a means to an end and not an end in and of themselves."[4] The degree of US need for Australia can change. Questions about the security relationship with the United States as a foundation stone for the policy need to be aired and investigated.

Second, questions can be raised about the policy conclusions inferred from the premises. It has been argued elsewhere but not at this seminar that if one accepts the assessment of threats to Australia contained in the Defence White Paper, then the valid conclusion to be drawn is that Australia's defence plans are inappropriate. Little threat should mean that Australia does not need the military force projection capabilities that the White Paper declares will be developed. (This is very different from views expressed at this seminar that Australia has too limited a conception of its area of strategic interest.) Plans for a capability to project force are seen as an illogical response to a non-threatening environment. The policy conclusion inferred by the Minister of Defence is a non-sequitur, a logical error. Linked to this argument could be accusations that the opportunity costs of the policy are high, that education, social services, and so on, contribute to the security of Australia and are inadequately funded because of the policy's diversion of funds to military spending to meet a non-existent threat. Differences in the policy conclusions inferred from the same premise of the threat environment reflect, in part, different assumptions about the nature of international relations. Is the international environment more benign, states more economically interdependent, more oriented toward their own domestic affairs, less aggressive than seems to be assumed by the policy? While I do not now want to take stand on this issue one way or the other, it is important to raise this here as a question.

Third, there are questions that need to be raised about whether the analysis that went into making the policy is complete or not. I doubt it. Note two of the ways in which the analysis is incomplete.

To begin with, the policy appears to be inadequately attuned to the fact that Australian security is part of a larger process of interactions among states. Other states will react to Australian defence measures. What is missing is the placement of the policy within the context of other states' reactions in an interaction process. Critics of the policy sometimes fail to take this larger view, also, Admiral Robertson in Chapter 3, for example, claims that "any nation possessing a submarine force of only modest size could pose us a most serious problem as could the use of mines, surface raiders, or, in some areas—aircraft." He expresses concern at Indian naval developments. Yet, Australia has a submarine force, and this force could be interpreted sometime in the future by leaders of another state as posing a threat to their country. Australia's strike force capabilities pose a potential threat to others, and the implications of Australia's military forces for others needs to be appreciated. It can affect how they conduct their relations with Australia. In part this is recognized. The Minister of Defence notes that one benefit of Australia's military capabilities will be some ability to influence other states. Frank Broeze, however, wonders if the configuration of Australia's military forces, for example, submarines, is appropriate for achieving political objectives. And, the consequences of the policy may be unintended. "Because the behaviour of states is interconnected, their goals conflict, and none of them is strong enough to control all the others, states' actions often produce unintended consequences," Jervis has observed. "Behaviour frequently yields results that are opposite from, or at a tangent to, those sought and predicted."[5] What is missing in the analysis is an appreciation of the dualistic nature of military forces; they are both a reaction to and a contributor toward conflict. "Modern armaments and military plans are a response to basic international conflicts," Thomas Schelling and Morton Halperin have noted. "It is also true that the size and character of military forces are an important determinant of national fears and anxieties, and of the military incentives of our potential enemies. There is a feedback between our military forces and the conflicts that they simultaneously reflect and influence."[6] Australian military capabilities and deployments can pose problems for other states, and that may adversely affect political relations. Military capabilities could be dysfunctional to the larger political objectives they should be designed to serve.

Another way the policy seems incomplete is related to what has just been said. There seems to be missing a core policy for relations with other states that gives direction to the policy we have been discussing. The policy seems to teeter on the edge of a black hole where there should be, but is not, an overarching policy that defines Australian security needs, goals, and actions in relations with other states. The policy we have been discussing should be subordinate to it, drawing sustenance and purpose from it.

Defence is part of a larger problem that needs to be addressed in its totality, with military instruments integrated with political and economic tools to achieve the larger objective. What is lacking is strategy, an overarching plan on how to use military instruments to achieve political objectives in Australia's relations with other states.

NOTES

1. Barry Buzan, **An Introduction to Strategic Studies: Military Technology and International Relations** (London: Macmillan, 1987) p.10.
2. Robert Jervis, "Hypotheses on Misperception", ed. Klaus Knorr, **Power, Strategy and Security** (Princeton: N.J.: Princeton University Press, 1983) p.161.
3. Alexander George, "Ideology and International Relations: A Conceptual Analysis", **Jerusalem Journal of International Relations,** 9(1):12, 1987.
4. Ibid.
5. Robert Jervis, "Systems Theories and Diplomatic History", ed. Paul Gordon Lauren, **Diplomacy: New Approaches in History, Theory and Policy** (New York: Free Press, 1979) p.216.
6. Thomas C. Schelling and Morton H. Halperin, **Strategy and Arms Control** (Washington, D.C.: Pergamon—Brassey's, 1985) p.4.

CHAPTER 4

Strategic Developments in the Indian and South Pacific Ocean Regions

K. Subrahmanyam

The strategic environment of any region of this small space station, called earth, which can be circled by a satellite in 90 minutes is influenced by the relationship between the two global powers, its superimposition on the regional developments and the developing techno-strategic factors both currently in progress and anticipated in the foreseeable future. For those who view the entire international system as a zero sum game there is no region in the world which they can afford to ignore as not of strategic relevance. Hence fishing agreements of some small South Pacific island states or attitude towards nuclear weapons by some 13000 people of Palau in Micronesia attract attention in Washington and Moscow. While perhaps some countries and some regions can claim that they do not anticipate a military threat it is difficult for any nation to assert that they can escape from the attention or pressures of various kinds of the primary hegemonic power of the world, the U.S. and to a lesser but yet significant extent, the secondary hegemonic power, the USSR. This is particularly true when the two major powers agree on certain rules of the game in regard to their mutual interaction in Europe and in regard to Japan. The second cold war which followed the detente in Europe was mostly a rivalry of the two great powers in the developing world. While there is ample ground for optimism that the second detente may follow the second cold war it will be overly optimistic to predict that the second detente will embrace the entire globe and there will be no more interventionism on the part of the two global powers in the ongoing turbulence of the developing world. All tension areas—Central America, Horn of Africa, Lebanon and

West Bank, Iran-Iraq war, the insurgencies in Afghanistan and Kampuchea, the instability in the Southern African region and numerous other local intra-state conflicts are all in the developing world and there is none in which either or both global powers have not evinced their interventionary proclivity, either direct or indirect.

Recently a bipartisan Commission of 13 eminent strategists under the co-chairmanship of Fred C. Ikle and Albert Wohlstetter have brought out a report on the American long term integrated strategy-titled "Discriminate Deterrence".[1] The Commission was reportedly conceived on a bipartisan basis so that its assessment would be acceptable to the next Administration irrespective of its being Democratic or Republican. The report is meant to guide the U.S. defence planning at least twenty years into the future. In the very first chapter the report draws attention to the possibility of the rise of Japan and China as potential military powers, even overtaking the Soviet Union by year 2010, and postulates that a world with three or four major global military powers would confront U.S. strategic planners with a far more complicated environment. There appears to be an unstated assumption of Western Europe as the fifth potential military power. It should interest Australians that four out of five potential military powers will be in the Pacific basin.

There is a further assumption in the report that India, Brazil, South and North Korea and Egypt will continue to build sizeable arms industries and understandably enough Israel has not been mentioned. Again it is of interest to note that five of these countries are in the Pacific and the Indian Ocean regions. The possibility of further nuclear proliferation is touched upon with some satisfaction that apart from five avowed nuclear weapon powers the other countries are engaged in nuclear weapon development only furtively. It is however conceded that the arsenals of the lesser powers will make it more difficult for the super powers to intervene in regional wars and the U.S. ability to support its allies around the world will increasingly be called into question. American intervention in Third World conflicts will generally require far more co-operation from Third World countries and will call for use of most sophisticated weapons. The report further stresses the diminishing ability of the U.S. to gain agreement for timely access including bases and overflight rights to areas threatened by Soviet aggression. Though the report refers to the possibility of Japan and China emerging as major powers it treats only the USSR as the potential adversary. The next two chapters are devoted to Third World conflicts and U.S. interests and wars on the Soviet periphery. The order in chaptering would suggest that the authors consider the above two contingencies as far more likely than the extreme threats which are dealt with later.

The authors acknowledge that in the past forty years all the wars in which the United States had been involved had occurred in the Third World. They are of the view that though such wars are less threatening than a war with the Soviet Union yet they can undermine the U.S. ability to defend its most vital interests. They advocate that the U.S. should be in a position to deal with low intensity conflicts in the developing world. For this purpose while generally avoiding getting involved in situations as direct combatants the U.S. should support anti Communist insurgencies. An effective way of carrying out this task is for the U.S. to work with its Third World allies at developing "co-operative forces". In the Third World, no less than in developed countries U.S. strategy should seek to maximise its technological advantages.

While we have the benefit of the views of the bipartisan U.S. Community of Strategists we do not have similar assessments of other major powers, China, Japan and USSR whose future plans will have a profound impact on the South Pacific and the Indian Ocean regions. The "Discriminate Deterrence" does mention in passing that a Japanese decision to help in the development of Soviet technology could help to increase the Soviet military potential. Even if Japan does not attempt to match its military potential to its economic strength it will be in a position to influence the strategic environment simply by its investment decisions. While the report mentions the possibility of China becoming one of the superpowers it also envisages large uncertainties in regard to China's future.

The present American exercise recalls to one's mind the reports of the "Committee on Present Danger" and the "High Frontier" Foundation which subsequently got translated into actual U.S. defence policies. No doubt the latest U.S. Budget proposals for fiscal year 1989 marks a slow down in spending on defence. But the impact of the report on "Discriminate Deterrence" will be felt in the rest of the world and particularly in Moscow, Beijing, Tokyo, and the European capitals. The initial reaction of European strategists (Messrs. Michael Howard, Karl Kaiser, Lawrence Freedman) has not been very enthusiastic. While it is not the purpose to treat the document as established U.S. policy it does provide tentative guidelines for developing an analytical framework for the developments in the Indian Ocean and South Pacific regions.

Yet another set of pronouncements relevant for our analysis are Gorbachev's Vladivostock speech of July 1986, his Murmansk speech, and the declaration he issued along with the Indian Prime Minister Rajiv Gandhi in November 1986. It is not proposed to overlook the basic factor in international relations that there are always gaps between declaratory policies and practice. The history of the last four decades demonstrates very clearly that in spite of all its economic constraints the Soviet Union has always tried to catch up with the U.S. weaponry after a certain time lag. Gorbachev looks forward to a nonviolent and nuclear free world. He is prepared to offer asymmetric cuts (provided the other side will agree to similar ones where it has disproportionate superiority) in conventional forces. He advocates a Nordic nuclear weapons free zone and an arms control regime for the Arctic. He is eager to join the Pacific Basin Economic Cooperation Advisory Council, improve relations with China, Japan and South East Asia and reduce competitive naval presences in the Pacific. The Soviet Union does not gloss over the hard fact that it has been stagnating economically and technologically. It wants to integrate itself increasingly with global institutions like GATT and needs foreign investments and technology to carry through its **Perestroika.**

The U.S. too is in economic difficulties and so is the rest of the world. For the first time in ten years the U.S. defence budget has been cut down from the earlier planned figure and the outlook for the next few years does not look optimistic. Part of their flotilla from the Gulf is being withdrawn to effect savings. The budgetary deficit does not show signs of rapid decline nor the balance of payments. Consequently it is reasonable to anticipate that there will be significant pressures to keep down the growth of U.S. defence budget in the next few years.

In Western Europe while there is a growing volume of public opinion in favour of West European self reliant defence, indicated by the increasing French-German collaboration, European efforts in respect of outer space, emphasis on mutual reduction of conventional forces, there is significant division of opinion on removal of short range nuclear missiles especially from West Germany and in regard to modernisation of shorter range nuclear weaponry. While Western Europe has done comparatively better economically than the U.S. there is reluctance to accept an increased defence burden. There are also strong pressures for forging closer economic links with the USSR and Eastern Europe for mutual economic benefit. Even the "Discriminate Deterrence" report considers an attack on Europe by the USSR as being in the extreme range of contingencies.

The Japanese defence budget is growing especially with the value of the yen going up. For the same amount of yens the Japanese will be able to buy more US and West European defence equipment and technology. The US, despite the concerns in China and South East Asia, is pressing Japan to assume greater defence responsibilities. At present there is a certain amount of unnatural discordance between the Japanese economic and technological power and military power. One wonders whether this state of affairs can continue for long. In spite of a slight downfall in the Japanese balance of trade advantage vis a vis US in 1987 and the value of the yen going up there is a point of view, expressed among others by the Prime Minister of Malaysia, Dt. Mahathir Mohammed in his speech to the Hong Kong bankers in 1985 that the primary conflict in the Pacific basin will not be between US and USSR or China-USSR or China-USA but the economic and technological competition between Japan and the USA.

The hegemonic power of US has been declining steadily over the years. While the Soviet Union has been the military counter-vailing factor the US has lost out technologically to Japan and Western Europe, agriculturally to Western Europe and countries like Canada, Australia, Argentina, India and China and politically to the developing world. This diffusion of power away from the US in different directions and not to a single rival has ensured that the US-USSR conflict did not result in combat. Nuclear weapons are yet another contributing factor and for the first time perhaps in history there are two navies operating globally cheek by jowl without daring to risk a conflict to determine their relative status of power.

The Chinese have perhaps slowed down their military spending though their published figures (as accepted even in the West) lack total credibility. China cannot maintain an armed force two and a half times India's, have a significant nuclear arsenal, modernise their forces all at a cost which is less than India's defence budget. Like many other statistics in respect of China their defence budget figures have to be taken with a trowel full of salt. Even the Ikle report refers to uncertainties in respect of China. While China's economic and military power are growing its problems are not lessening in number. One wonders whether the Hong Kong merger will be benign or cancerous for the Chinese system and is entitled to speculate what impact it will have on non-Han minorities such as Tibetans, Uighurs, Mongols etc. If there can be one nation and two systems among the Hans themselves (Hong Kong is mostly Han Chinese) there can be demands why there should not be different systems (more autonomy) for the non-Han people. The Taiwan issue is slowly drifting toward the two China solution with potential for violent differences between China on one hand, Japan and US on the other. If there are racial explosions in South-east Asia, China would be perceived as a malign factor. The future Army-Party relationship when Deng disappears from the scene is a question mark and one cannot be optimistic that technocrats like Zhao Zhiang and Li Peng could exercise the degree of control over the PLA which the last surviving Commissar of Revolutionary Chinese Army Deng Xiao Peng was able to do.

The Chinese naval power is growing. It is not the Soviet anti-shipping missiles but the Chinese Silkworm which is a prominent factor in the Gulf war today. The Chinese navy has entered the Indian Ocean and visited Pakistan, Sri Lanka, Bangladesh and held a signal exercise with the US fleet in the South China Sea in January 1987. There are collaborative military projects on the anvil with Pakistan for fitting in an American engine, avionics and weaponry to a Chinese air frame. There have been reports of Chinese transfer of submarines to Thailand being under discussion. China has emerged as one of the leading major arms suppliers to the Indian Ocean littoral countries. There has always been speculation where the Chinese will deploy their nuclear missile submarines in its second strike role vis a vis USSR. The most convenient area of deployment will be the North Arabian Sea and a nuclear Pakistan may be in a position to offer a home port to Chinese nuclear missile submarines without worrying unduly about Soviet pressure.

The US has already established a central command in the Indian Ocean area with contingent jurisdiction over nineteen countries from Pakistan to Kenya and deploys on a continuous basis a carrier task force which as a standard procedure will have one or two hunter killer nuclear submarines accompanying it for protection. The Ikle report, even while emphasising the growing urgent need for co-operative forces in the Third World (Pakistan, Saudi Arabia, Egypt being the primary examples) says nothing to generate an impression that the US has any intention of reducing its commitments in the Indian Ocean area. If all the recent debates are any clue there is a strongly held view that the Gulf region should not be left to the Soviet Union and the US should have a superior naval presence. The investment in the build up in the Diego Garcia base and the emphasis in the Ikle Report on access to various regions of the developing world would tend to indicate the US has no intention of reducing its presence in the Indian Ocean region. The prepositioned supply flotilla around Diego Garcia is yet another indication of their contingency plans.

The Soviet Union needs the Indian Ocean presence for four reasons:

- It forms the passage connecting its Atlantic and Black Sea fleets with the Pacific fleets.
- The Arabian Sea is within striking distance for its Asian Republics.
- It has to maintain space operations related ships in South West quadrant of the Indian Ocean as unlike the US it has no land based satellite monitoring and commanding stations in Southern hemisphere (US has Pine Gap, Nurrungar in Australia and Victoria Station in Seychelles).
- It has to maintain credibility with friendly states such as Ethiopia and Mozambique.

As compared to US presence the Soviet presence is much smaller. According to **Military Balance 1987-88** the US presence in the Indian Ocean comprised of:

- Detachments from Seventh and Second fleets (11000 personnel)
- Base Diego Garcia (1,700)
- 1 carrier battle group (6 surface combatants)

- 5 MPS (eqpt for one MAB)
- 1 command ship, usually 4 destroyers/frigates in the Gulf
- Temporary deployment 1 cruiser and 4 escorts in July 1987.

The Soviet regular deployments included on an average 0-1 submarine, 1-2 principal, 1-2 minor surface combatants, 1 amphibious, and 6-8 support ships.

Very often arguments are put forward that a strong western naval presence is essential in the Indian Ocean to counter-balance the massive Soviet power in the land mass in Eurasia. If this logic were to be extended a similar counter naval presence to balance US continental power in the Caribbean and the Chinese power in the East and South China seas will become rational. Such arguments have an element of self righteousness and egocentric moralising posture.

The second strongest external power in the Indian Ocean is not the Soviet Union but France. According to **Military Balance 1987-88** South Indian Ocean command embracing Mayotte, and La Reunion has 3,300 personnel including 1 marine infantry regiment, 2 infantry companies, 1 air transport unit, 5 frigates, 2 minor combatants, 2 amphibious and 4 support ships, 1 Atlantic MR aircraft. In addition in Djibouti France maintains 4,000 personnel comprising 2 regiments, 2 light tank squadrons, 1 mixed armoured squadron, 2 motor infantry companies, 1 artillery battery, one AA artillery battery, 1 pioneer company, 5 attack and 5 medium transport helicopters, 1 squadron with 7 Mirage IIIC aircraft, one C-160 transport aircraft, 3 Alouette II helicopters.

The British have in the Indian Ocean 1 destroyer, 2 frigates, 1 support ship and one naval party and one marine detachment in Diego Garcia.

The Indian Ocean which used to be nuclear free when the so-called Nonproliferation Treaty was signed can no longer be considered so. The US aircraft carriers have as their standard equipment nuclear weapons and many of their combat ships are believed to carry nuclear weapons. P3C maritime recce aircraft which operate regularly over the Indian Ocean can carry nuclear depth charges. Diego Garcia can take on its airfield B-52 and F-111 aircraft. One of the basic principles of arms control agreements is that platforms that have been tested to carry nuclear weapons should be presumed to be so deployed. The position in regard to the French, British and Soviet ships should also be considered in an analogous manner.

Apart from these nuclear weapons at sea, Senator Glenn said on the Senate Floor on 11 December 1987, "There is no intelligence operation in the world that does not believe that Israel has nuclear weapons. That is no secret". It is often overlooked that Israel with its port Eilat in the Gulf of Aqaba is an Indian Ocean littoral state. The US Administration has now conceded that Pakistan has the technical capability to produce nuclear weapons. Given eight and a half years of waiver of the Symington Amendment Pakistanis are not so backward that they could not have reached the capability to put together a nuclear weapon. Dr A.Q. Khan, the head of Kahtu establishment, admitted their possession of the weapon to an Indian journalist in the presence of a reputed Pakistani Editor who confirmed the story and got sacked.

Today four of the five avowed nuclear weapon powers and two littoral states with clandestine nuclear arsenals and a third state, India, which has carried out a nuclear test and can go nuclear at short notice, are present in the Indian Ocean. If China is to join, that would make it the eighth nuclear weapon nation operating in the Indian Ocean. So much for nonproliferation and the declaration that the Indian Ocean should be a peace zone. There are in addition other nations like Australia which provide access facilities to nuclear weapon carriers and have on their soil the infra-structure for command, control, communication and intelligence facilities to fight a nuclear war.

The position in respect of South Africa is somewhat ambivalent. While the Ruina-Garwin panel had declared that the flash of September 1979 which was detected by the US VELA satellite is a zoo event, a new book by an Israeli author, Benjamin Beit Hallahami, titled **Israeli Connection** claims that it was a joint South African and Israeli test of a nuclear shell fired from a 155 mm Armscor gun.[2] There are unconfirmed reports emanating from Paris that France intends to shift its nuclear test site from Mururoa Atoll to one of the South Indian Ocean islands under its jurisdiction.

Apart from the nuclear aspect, new technological developments have taken place in naval warfare that have not been subjected to detailed analysis in published literature. The British Navy was able to bottle up the entire Argentine Navy in its ports after one of its nuclear propelled hunter killer submarines torpedoed *General Belgrano*, the Argentine cruiser. Various navies of the world have drawn appropriate conclusions from the South Atlantic War. The Canadians have published their defence White Paper in which they have outlined plans to acquire a number of nuclear propelled submarines, not to keep the Soviets out of their waters, but the Americans who do not respect the Canadian sovereignty over their Arctic waters. The British and the French are looking for lucrative contracts and even the U.S. has offered technology transfer. Brazil and Argentina have announced plans to build nuclear propelled submarines. The Soviet Union has transferred to India a Victor class nuclear propelled submarine. The so-called NPT does not cover transfer of reactors for nonpeaceful purposes and therefore nuclear submarines can sail through the so-called NPT. One may expect a certain proliferation of nuclear propelled submarines now that one of the high priests of the nonproliferation cult (Canada) itself is opting for it.

Another worrisome development is the submarine launched missiles—ranging from Exocets and Harpoons to Cruise missiles carrying conventional warheads several hundred miles. Until now a submarine was a threat only to naval targets, but no longer. Today submarines can fire missiles from several scores of miles to several hundreds of miles from the coast, to destroy military and valuable industrial targets such as nuclear power stations and petrochemical complexes, thereby causing Chernobyls and Bhopals. Consequently anti-submarine warfare has acquired new dimensions. It is not enough to convoy one's merchant fleet and keep vigilant anti-submarine watch in regard to one's own fleet. It is necessary to ensure that a nation's coastal targets are not threatened by a Harpoon or analogous missile. In turn this requires anti-submarine operations in the air (with maritime recce and strike aircraft), on the sea surface with destroyers and aircapable ships (small aircraft carriers carrying anti-submarine patrol helicopters and Harrier aircraft), quiet hunter killer submarines, and most effective of all, the deep water operating, fast running, nuclear propelled submarine. This is the strategic planning perspective which has led to the Indian Navy acquiring Tu 142 M maritime recce and strike aircraft, the second aircraft carrier with Harriers and Seakings, the German Type 1500-HDW submarine and the Victor class nuclear propelled submarine.

These are primarily intended to bottle up the Pakistani Navy which is equipped with Agosta and Daphne submarines, and six US Gearing class destroyers which are equipped with Harpoon missiles. (They have on order 2 British type 23 and 2 Dutch M class frigates). In addition, given the operation of nuclear hunter killer submarines of nuclear weapons in the Indian Ocean, it is also essential to keep watch over their activities around the coastal waters of India. The neighbours of India have in all 17 submarines at present (Pakistan—2 Agostas, 4 Daphnes and 2 S x 404 midget submarines; Indonesia—2 type 1300 class submarines and one more is on order; and Iran has on order 6 type 1200 submarines).

The deep diving mini submarines constitute a new dimension in naval threat. Some of them can operate down to three to four miles depth and can be used to damage off-shore oil installations, to listen to submarine cable traffic etc. According to a report in the **Independent** (London) Pakistan and Libya have acquired such submarines.[3] India has off-shore oil installations in Bombay High basin and is developing the off-shore oil wells of Cauvery, Godavari, and Krishna basins around Andamans.

It used to be argued that one of the reasons for the presence of foreign navies in the Indian Ocean was protection of oil lanes, and by implication the Soviet Union used to be considered as the primary threat. Now the Soviet Union is leasing its tankers to Kuwait to take oil out of the Gulf to the Western industrialised nations and Soviet warships are escorting other oil carrying vessels. On the other, hand maximum damage to oil tankers has been caused by the Exocet missiles made in France and launched by Mirages, and Etendard aircraft supplied by France to Iraqis. The Iranians are posing a threat too with Silkworm missiles manufactured in China. While it is unreasonable to expect the Western strategists to confess that their earlier assumptions were wholly wrong, it is incomprehensible that the same discredited arguments are still being used even in recent assessments. There is no discussion of how to deal with the French and Chinese threats to oil supplies to Western industrial countries. It is now quite clear that the presence of external navies in the Indian Ocean is not primarily intended to safeguard international oil supplies but to intervene selectively on behalf of favoured clients. It has been alleged that during the Iran-Iraq War intelligence was supplied selectively and appropriately doctored to both sides by the US. This kind of intelligence sharing with favoured client states making use of their naval presence in the Indian Ocean is one of the concerns of the Indian Navy.

India had been subjected to an exercise of force without war in 1971 when the task force 74 headed by the nuclear powered carrier USS Enterprise tried to intervene—though it proved to be too late—in the last stages of the war in Bangladesh. Nuclear propelled submarines with ability to lay in wait quietly for long periods of time provide some minimal deterrence against such interventionism.

India also has some obligations towards the island nations of the Indian Ocean which look to India for security. At present the Indian Army is carrying out a counter insurgency operation against Tamil secessionists in Sri Lanka at the request of the Sri Lankan Government. This is not the first time India has had to go to the help of Sri Lanka. In 1971 the then Government of Sri Lanka, headed by Mrs Sirimavo Bandaranaike (now in opposition), and faced with an insurgency by JVP (Janata Vimukti Peramuna—People's Liberation Front), asked for Indian help. India sent 5,000 troops and the Indian Navy sealed off Sri Lanka to prevent any external help reaching the insurgents.

India also has island possessions to defend. Andamans and Nicobars contain several hundreds of thousands of Indian population who elect a member to the Indian Parliament. So also the populations in Minicoy and Lakshadweep islands in the Arabian Sea. The former archipelago is separated from India by 700 miles but is close to other nations. The Indian Navy is structured to carry out the defence of these islands, among other tasks.

There have been coup attempts in the island nations of the Indian Ocean. In Seychelles a few years back a band of mercenaries led by Colonel Mad Mike Hoare attempted a coup, and when it was foiled because of its detection in time, they hijacked an Air India jumbo jet. In 1986 during the Non-aligned Summit at Harare the Seychelles President Rene had to rush back to the Seychelles because of intelligence that this defence minister was plotting a coup. The Indian Prime Minister lent his aircraft to enable him to fly back to forestall the coup. Mauritius is increasingly reliant on India for its security needs.

Out of four quadrants of the Indian Ocean there are considerable naval activities in three of them—North West, North East and South West. The relatively quiescent quadrant is the South East abutting Australia. The recent Australian assessment based on Mr Paul Dibb's review and the Australian White Paper that Australia does not face any imminent military threat is indisputable. At the same time, according to a BBC report, Australia intends to intensify its military cooperation with South East Asian countries and hold exercises with some of them.[4] The Australian perspective which used to be directed more towards South East and East Asia when Japan and then China were considered potential adversaries, has tended to turn more towards the South Pacific. This is only logical since 14 new nations have emerged out of the decolonisation process. Until decolonisation took place, since these islands were under British and Australian protection, they posed neither military nor political problems. With the islands becoming sovereign nations this position has radically changed. This is now recognised in Australia. The problem is not likely to be so much military as political as evidenced by the recent developments in Fiji, New Caledonia, in regard to the Rarotonga Treaty, the attempts of some of the island nations to establish relations with Libya or the Soviet Union and possible expansion of Japanese influence. Some of these developments also tended to highlight that Australia can no longer take for granted that its own assessments of situations in these island nations will completely go along with those of the United States. The recent visit of the French Defence Minister did not bring about a meeting of the minds. The ANZUS Treaty is under great strain in the light of the attitude adopted by the US towards New Zealand. France has some island possessions in the South Indian Ocean too. While perhaps no nationalist upsurge is to be expected in Mayotte, New Amsterdam, Kergulen, and the Crozet islands the same cannot be said about La Reunion. Therefore in political terms the Australian concerns are likely to be more focussed on the South Pacific, the French possessions in the Indian Ocean and to the neighbours in the immediate north, Indonesia and Papua New Guinea, none of which is likely to cause serious military concern.

Having said that, attention has to be drawn to a likely new technological development which at present is only a concept but has potentiality of developing into a major concern for security of nations. Some Western strategists have argued that with the signing of the START the US will have to reduce its submarine borne missiles drastically and also reduce its missile carrying submarines. Gorbachev is also pressing for a ceiling on nuclear warhead carrying cruise missiles. All these proposals will lead to a reduction in the number of missile carrying submarines since at present most of them have multiple warheaded missiles. In turn it would mean the number of targets which an adversary has to locate gets limited. The strategists of one school argue that this is not a desirable thing and in their view it would be a less stabilised situation. Therefore they favour given a reduced ceiling in terms of warheads, that the multiple warheaded missiles should be replaced by single warheaded missiles (in US the project for the single warhead land based missile is called Midgetman, which idea goes back to the Scrowcroft Commission). Now one strategist has proposed that the same principle should be extended to submarine launched missiles, and the present Trident submarine carrying 192 warheads should be replaced by smaller submarines carrying not more than 20 warheads each.[5] This particular strategist advocates smaller nuclear arsenals for both sides. On the other hand there is a possibility of the idea being picked up in respect of smaller submarines with a limited number of warheads without the arsenal of 6000 warheads on each side being reduced. The idea may also spread to other avowed and not avowed nuclear weapon nations. That might lead to a larger number of hunter killer submarines being built with various kinds of stand off weaponry. In other words the world can see a submarine proliferation.

The larger the number of missile carrying submarines the logic will be in favour of their being spread over wider areas of the Ocean further away from areas where relatively more effective anti-submarine measures can be adopted or at least made more costly and difficult. In this context the Southern oceans may come to play a more significant role. Recently Admiral Hays, C. in C. Pacific Command, said in a British Channel 4 television programme explaining his opposition to the Rarotonga Nuclear Weapon Free Zone Treaty, that once one nuclear weapon free zone is accepted then there will be pressures for more and more of them and that was not acceptable.[6] This explains the US opposition to nuclear weapon free zones in the South Pacific, South East Asia, Balkans, and the Nordic area and affects the credibility of one nuclear weapon free zone they have endorsed—the Latin

American one which has not been brought into force by more than 50 per cent of the designated area—by Argentina, Brazil, Chile and Cuba.

There is yet another factor which may make the Southern oceans strategically more important in the future though certain recent developments have tended to push this factor into the background for the present. There is always the risk of its getting revived. This relates to anti satellite warfare which is bound to become an essential component of the Star Wars programme if that is to progress beyond the stage of laboratory experimentation and be ready for deployment.

A Star Wars programme necessarily implies monitoring from space the adversary's missiles and submarines and attempts to destroy those missiles at boost phase and the warheads at mid-course phase and terminal phase. If at all one visualises the extreme contingency of a nation starting a large scale nuclear war it must attempt to destroy the monitoring systems, namely the satellites and therefore an anti-satellite warfare capability is implicit in the assumptions on which Star Wars defences are to be built. As of today the satellites—especially the Soviet satellites—come low over the Southern Hemisphere in their polar orbits so that they can have a longer dwell time over the Northern Hemisphere in their elliptical orbit, as most of the targets they have to keep under watch are in the Northern Hemisphere. Therefore anyone attempting to destroy the satellites in orbit would try shooting them down while they are orbiting low—over the Southern oceans.

Trials have been conducted using a F-15 aircraft platform and a MHV (Miniature Homing Vehicle) in an anti-satellite role, though the Congress has now prohibited further tests. It is anybody's guess what future Administrations and Congresses will do. The Soviet offer to have a treaty to ban development of anti-satellite weapons has been rejected. In a sense the Star Wars programme for terminal phase and mid-course interceptions will provide the necessary technology for anti-satellite capability too. The report on "Discriminate Deterrence" emphasises, among various other points on space capabilities, the need for "a capability in wartime to disable hostile satellites at all altitudes and to attack the ground elements of enemy space systems with non-nuclear space systems".[7]

These are some of the general considerations which, as a strategist, I would expect should influence Australian strategic thinking, though I would readily disqualify myself in respect of my knowledge, competence and understanding, both subjective and objective, of Australia self-perceptions to pronounce on Australian formulation of their future strategy and much less on their force composition. I must confess that Australia has not figured in our security calculations except as a benign factor which helped us in 1962 and with whose forces the British Indian Army had fought as comrades in various global theatres in the 1914-1918 and 1939-45 wars. Given Australia's geographic location, and its neighbourhood, it would appear that any view which focuses exclusively on US-Soviet rivalry ignoring the possible roles of China and Japan and the possible turbulence in the South Pacific islands, would be a limited one.

There is one factor on which I hope to gain further understanding during the deliberation of this conference. How does Australia reconcile its objection to the French tests in Mururoa Atoll, its membership in Rarotonga Treaty, with its voting in the UN on the non-aligned resolutions seeking the ultimate ban on the use and threat of use of nuclear weapons (which has obtained more than 132 votes in favour including that of China and the USSR and is opposed only by NATO nations [except Greece] and Australia)?

If legitimacy of nuclear weapons as instruments of international power is conceded, then how does one object to France's right to conduct its own nuclear tests or for that matter US, Soviet, Chinese and British weapon tests? I am somewhat puzzled by Australian objection to French tests while endorsing the legitimacy of nuclear weapons and providing the nuclear warfighting infra-structure for the USA in Australia as a piece of real estate. How does Australia expect the Soviet Union not to be active in and around its waters so long as Australia is a vital link in the US nuclear warfighting command, control, communication and intelligence chain?

I am not endorsing the Soviet activity but only pointing out the logic of it. For a person coming from the non-aligned world and not being quite familiar with the intricacies of Australian strategic thinking it would appear that New Zealand's policy is internally more consistent than that of Australia. This is not intended as a criticism but only an attempt at understanding the

Australian policy better.

NOTES

1. "Discriminate Deterrence: Report of the Commission on Integrated Long-Term Strategy," January 1988.
2. Quoted in the **Guardian** (London), 14 January 1988.
3. **Independent** (London), 1 January 1988.
4. BBC, "24 Hours", 1310 GMT, 23 February 1988.
5. **International Herald Tribune**, 12 January 1988.
6. **Dispatches**, 19 February 1988.
7. I am grateful to Air Commodore Jasjit Singh, my former colleague and presently Director, Institute for Defence Studies and Analyses for focussing on the importance of Southern oceans in ASAT operation.

Comments

Mohammed Ayoob

The analysis that Subrahmanyam has presented is, in many ways, a good antidote to the narrowly based analyses of the sort that we had heard earlier in this conference about what was happening in the Indian Ocean. It is a good antidote because it puts the Indian Ocean in its proper strategic context and forcefully makes the point that the Indian Ocean is not an isolated strategic or political theatre which can be studied without reference to contiguous regions or to the changing configurations of power throughout the globe. What happens in the Asia-Pacific region in terms of the changes that are now being introduced, and are likely to be accelerated during the next decade, impinges upon the balance of power in the Indian Ocean and would impinge upon it in an even bigger way in future. Therefore, it would be foolhardy for us to analyse either the events in the Indian Ocean, whether naval or otherwise, or the requirements of Australian security in relation to the Indian Ocean primarily from a narrow naval point of view because an exclusively naval point of view can lead us to distorted conclusions. The fact that Subrahmanyam has been able to put the developments in the Indian Ocean region in their proper strategic context has provided a great deal of food for thought and it is something that can be built upon in future studies of Australian foreign and defence policy.

One main point that has emerged from his paper which has helped to broaden the discussion is his emphasis upon not merely the "balance of forces", that is, the overall military capabilities of the major powers around the Indian Ocean, or for that matter in the Asia-Pacific region, but on the "balance of power" in the Asia-Pacific region. This goes beyond merely an analysis of the balance of forces or military capabilities. It takes into account various other variables including technology, economic capabilities, diplomatic clout, etc. Therefore, it has helped us to move the discussion beyond the analysis of merely military factors.

As Subrahmanyam has very rightly pointed out with reference to the report under the title "Discriminate Deterrence", that was issued by thirteen eminent Americans not so long ago, the emergence of China and Japan as major actors in their own right in the Asia-Pacific region has brought about, and is likely to bring about in the next decade, fundamental changes to the configuration of power in this region and Australian and other Indian Ocean or Asian-Pacific security analysts would do well to take note of this fact.

The interaction of these two emerging powers, that are now in the process of coming into their own as autonomous actors, makes a major difference to the balance of power because while on the one hand, by and large, the strategic bipolarity between the two superpowers in terms of the global picture remains constant, the balance of power in the Asia-Pacific has begun to undergo change, and the region is becoming much more multipolar in character. Unlike in Europe, which had so far been the major centre of the cold war and where the East-West lines are clearly drawn and both the superpowers know where to stop and what limits not to overstep, the situation in the Asia-Pacific region is far more fluid. Here pieces are still in the process of falling into place and a much more genuine form of multipolarity can, therefore, be envisaged.

China has now emerged as a full-fledged autonomous actor. It had always had the ambitions to act autonomously of the two superpowers despite its alliance in the first decade after the revolution with the Soviet Union and its semi-alliance with the United States from about 1976 up to 1981/1982. Since 1982 the Chinese have announced that they are going to take a position which would be much more equidistant from the two superpowers, although they still tend to lean, for economic and technological as much as political reasons, to one side. In some sense they have emphasized the original definition of non-alignment, that non-alignment is not merely a mechanical equidistance from the two major poles of power, but that a nation like China, or for that matter India or any of the major non-aligned nations, has the right to take its own decisions based on its own interests and/or on the merits of a particular case.

The Japanese are in the process of following this same path towards autonomy and probably in a much bigger way because there is a fundamental difference between China and Japan. Japan is not merely a technological and economic superpower; in terms of the traits or characteristics of its political system it belongs to the First World of industrialized democracies. Therefore, both in terms of its technological and economic power and the consensus in Japanese society about fundamental issues of social and political organization it belongs to the First World in the sense that one cannot envisage major discontinuities in terms of this consensus which underpins the Japanese polity. Therefore, as an industrialized and developed power, it will follow more or less a unilinear course that would lead to the achievement of Japanese interests by and large as defined by the Japanese elite.

China does not fall in that category. China, despite the addition to its capabilities, and Subrahmanyam has given us an account of the expansion of its naval capabilities, of its missile capabilities, etc., is still primarily a Third World country in terms of its economy, and in terms of its political development, which is far from being certain or unilinear. This means that all the uncertainties attendant upon being a Third World country would continue to plague China for the next decade and beyond. The introduction of market forces into the Chinese economy has, in fact, made the situation in that country potentially even more volatile. Increasing economic liberalization exists in a state of acute tension with rigid political regimentation. This tension might lead to a major breakdown in the political consensus within the Chinese ruling elite and result in grave problems both for China itself and for its neighbours. Therefore, the course that China would chart out for itself can yet be subject to major upheavals and major changes which even the most perceptive analyst cannot fully foresee at this stage.

The other difference between China and Japan is that while China is a major regional power in its own right that can impinge upon the interests of the other regional powers, whether they be Vietnam, Indonesia, India, or even Australia, and which can have a major input into the process of change in configuration of power in the Asia-Pacific, Japan, once it takes the political decision to translate its tremendous economic and technological clout into political power and strategic capabilities, would be operating on a totally different level. It would be operating not merely at the level of the Asia-Pacific but of the globe. It would be a contender for power with the two dominant powers in the international system today and such an eventuality could destabilize, from the point of view of the superpowers, the entire picture in the Asia-Pacific region and in the international system as a whole. So we have a potential global power and a potential regionally dominant power in Japan and China, competing with each other, as well as competing with the Soviet Union and the United States in this increasingly multipolar balance of power in the Asia-Pacific region. This can have all sorts of unforeseen consequences for the security of the countries of the Indian Ocean littoral and of the Pacific littoral as well.

Subrahmanyan in one of his articles that I had read sometime ago had suggested that he sees the primary emerging conflict in the international system as one between the United States and Japan because of the economic competition between the two countries and because of the fact that the United States and the other industrialized countries, short of subverting the established pattern of industrial relations in Japan, would not be able to compete with Japanese productivity.

However, my favourite scenario for the Asia-Pacific region is slightly different. While I take into account the technological and economic dimensions of Japanese-American relations which have led him to this conclusion, and while I think that that competition will continue, I still feel that American thinking regarding this part of the world, while taking into account the Japanese techno-economic challenge, would still be, by and large, determined by Washington's perceptions of strategic bipolarity. If that continues to be the case then, with the increasing clout of Japan, Tokyo would be seen by Washington not merely, as the former Japanese Prime Minister Yasuhiro Nakasone had said, "an unsinkable aircraft carrier" but as an "indispensable aircraft carrier" in the Pacific in terms of overall Western strategy. This would mean that within the context of the Western alliance Japanese clout vis-a-vis Washington will increase dramatically and Japan would be in a position in the next ten or fifteen years to carve out a sub-sphere of influence for itself within the larger Asia-Pacific region and within the context of the Western alliance system. In this sub-sphere it would act in tandem with the United States for the preservation of the larger Western security interests but would be allowed a free hand to deal with local issues in the way it would want to in order to preserve or enhance its own interests. If that happens there would be a major clash of interests between Japan and China. Given China's own ambitions, given the history of Chinese suspicions of Japanese power, especially as it had been exercised before the Second World War and during that War, and given the fact that Chinese historical memories of Japanese expansionism are even more acute than their historical memories of Soviet expansionism, it could introduce all sorts of new variables in inter-state relations in the Asia-Pacific region. It might even accelerate the process of rapprochement between China and the Soviet Union, for if Japan is allowed a relatively free hand by the United States in the Asia-Pacific region the only power that China can turn to would be the Soviet Union.

This is one reason why regional powers in Asia, like India, Indonesia and Vietnam, who see China as the major regional threat to their own interests, would like to build up their own capabilities because of the uncertainties of the shifting alignments in the Asia-Pacific region over the next decade or two. Even those powers, like Vietnam and India, who are in one way or another on good terms with the Soviet Union but whose primary focus of strategic apprehension is China, would try to diversify their contacts and build up their own power because there is no certainty that the Sino-Soviet antagonism would continue into the 1990s. While a Sino-Soviet rapprochement may or may not be able to stem the Japanese tide in the Pacific it will have important consequences for countries like India, Indonesia and Vietnam in the Indian Ocean region because of the fact that China is perceived by them as the primary source of threat to themselves. I think it is in the context of these factors that Australian policy towards the Indian Ocean region needs to be formulated. It cannot be formulated, I would like to reiterate, in isolation from the larger Asia-Pacific theatre and the likely impact of growing Chinese power on the Asian balance of power, especially on the policies of the "regional influentials" like India, Indonesia and Vietnam, and of the likely impact of growing Japanese power on the balance of global power and on the Asia-Pacific region.

PART 3

Focus on the Persian Gulf: The United States and Australia

CHAPTER 5

US Military Build-up in the Persian Gulf: Limitations and Risks

Rasul B. Rais

Strengthening of military capabilities to project power rapidly and effectively to the Persian Gulf has emerged as one of the salient features of US strategy. Initiatives ranging from augmenting the naval presence to acquiring a wide network of bases for prepositioning equipment have been aimed at enabling the US forces to assume a direct security role. Linking regional stability to US military presence is a reversal of the Nixon Doctrine which attached greater significance to the role of regional powers in promoting security and restricted the US military power to supplemental tasks. Fundamental change in the security doctrine and structure of forces was guided both by regional imperatives as well as by Soviet behaviour. Firstly, the loss of Iran to anti-American fundamentalist Ayatollahs who appeared to be seeking the establishment of Islamic regimes in the neighbouring Gulf States raised the fears of much wider instability in the region. Secondly, the eruption of the Gulf War which does not seem about to end in the near future qualitatively changed the threat perceptions of pro-west Arab states. Thirdly, Soviet military intervention in Afghanistan introduced a new element into the strategic environment of South-West Asia.

Central concern of the US strategy is with how to maintain favourable political and security arrangements in this region in the face of escalatory potential of the Gulf war, and the destabilising threat of Iran's political and security doctrines.

To inspire and restore confidence in US power, President Carter revitalised American commitment to one of preventing the control of the Persian Gulf by a hostile power and equated such an attempt with an assault on the vital interests of the United States that would if necessary be repelled by military power.[1] Under this doctrine the US has attempted to acquire capability in the region to respond effectively to "threats across the entire spectrum of conflict".[2] The major assumption of US Gulf strategy is that its ability to play an effective security role would depend on massive build-up of military power. The central argument of this paper is that the "credible deterrence" which the US forces have attempted to establish in the Gulf might confront challenges which may not be manageable merely through achieving power projection capability or by holding a threat of punitive strike against the potential adversaries. How much forces would be enough to constitute credible deterrence or give the US forces capability to sustain a conflict is a question which finds no definite answer in a highly volatile, and complex threat environment of South-West Asia. An effective response would depend much on the identification of threats and challenges which is equally an elusive task. Perhaps, ranking of potential threats in order of their severity and likelihood would make the task of constituting appropriate forces relatively easy. The following sections will examine the combination of US forces, their operational capabilities and the limitations and risks involved in their application.

Military Build-up

To enhance its power projection capabilities in the Gulf, the United States has taken a number of concerted actions. First is the maintenance of strong military presence in the area which combines ability to conduct reconnaissance missions, undertake tactical air operations, establish sea control and capture strategic zones in the coastal areas of the target states. The United States has emerged as a dominant naval power in the Gulf with the regular deployment of an aircraft carrier battle group, eight frigates and destroyers, plus two cruisers that are equipped with sophisticated anti-aircraft system radars.[3] These forces have been designed and equipped to deal with local contingencies and hold their own at the start of a wider conflict until forces from the US and NATO bases in Europe are flown in.

Creation of rapid deployment forces was the second important initiative toward strengthening credibility of the US military build-up in the Persian Gulf. Roughly six months before the pronouncement of the Carter Doctrine, the Pentagon prepared a report (Wolfowitz report) in June 1979 on US force requirements in this region.[4] According to the Wolfowitz report, the US would have to deploy a good combination of forces-marines, airborne forces, air cavalry, tactical air, strong naval presence-to shore up power for potential involvements ranging from assisting the counter insurgency operations of the regional allies to full-scale military operations.[5] The fact that planning of an intervention force to meet threats in the Third World in general and the Indian Ocean region in particular was done much before the Soviet intervention in Afghanistan suggests that it was essentially in response to the Gulf situation. The Soviet action nevertheless hastened US contingency plans for the region.[6] When the United States planned the Rapid Deployment Joint Task Force (RDJFT) for the Gulf, it allocated one Marine Amphibious Force, three Army divisions (the 82nd Airborne, 101st Airmobile, and 24th Mechanised). Also, a variety of smaller combat and supporting units (200,000 men), seven tactical fighting wings (approximately 500 aircraft from the Air Force and Air National Guard) were assigned to the RDJFT.[7] Since its conversion into the Central Command (CENTCOM), the US forces designed to meet contingencies in the Gulf have grown to five Army and two Marine Corps divisions. Tactical Fighter wings have been increased to ten.[8]

The United States has taken three important initiatives towards enhancing the flexibility and combat effectiveness of the CENTCOM. Firstly, it has gradually increased its capacity to airlift appropriate combat weapons to the area of conflict. The US Air Force Fleet of 279 C-141s has received added capacity for inflight refueling. The purchase of KC-10 tankers has furthered increased refueling capability. The completion of the ongoing procurement of 50 C-5BS will significantly increase the size of outsize cargo fleet. Egypt, Morocco and some European allies have agreed to provide refueling facilities for US aircraft airlifting military equipment to the Persian Gulf.[9] The US Navy has also strengthened its sealift capability by acquiring 8 SL-7 fast deployment container ships. These ships with roll-on and roll-off features have the capacity to move a mechanised division to the Gulf in less than three weeks.[10] The option to mobilise the Merchant Marine and National Defense Reserve Fleet (NDFR) would give the US Navy enough cargo capacity to support major operations in the Gulf.

The second set of initiatives has focused on prepositioning military equipment close to the Persian Gulf. Two types of ships have been acquired by the US Navy to keep sufficient military hardware afloat in the region. First are the Near Term Prepositioning Ships (NTPS) which carry equipment for a Marine amphibious brigade and reserve stock for US Air Force fighter squadrons. The second type are about 12 Maritime Prepositioning Ships (MPS).[11] These ships have enough storage capacity for carrying sufficient supplies for three marine brigades and would support the CENTCOM operation of putting the men and material ashore.

Thirdly, to increase mobility and sufficient logistical support for its forces present in the region the United States has gained access to a wide network of air and naval facilities in Egypt, Kenya, Oman and Somalia.[12] Diego Garcia with steady expansion and improvement is capable of serving multipurpose functions. The base is capable of providing communications, storing CENTCOM equipment, and maritime surveillance. The problem of storing sufficient ammunition, equipment, fuel and food supplies for a period until fresh supplies from the US could be lifted by sea or air has been the weak link in US strategic planning for the Persian Gulf. With the access to facilities around the region and acquisition of 17 large container ships loaded with supplies the problem has been partly resolved. The US access to regional facilities would serve a variety of combat and support purposes:

- prepositioning of stocks and combat forces,
- rear staging,
- sea control,
- support airlift and sealift operations, and
- secure air and sea lines of communication by which to deploy and resupply forces.

Strengthening the self-defence capabilities of the Arab Gulf states through sale of appropriate weapons and bilateral, informal security linkages is an important component of US strategy. This policy is guided by three concerns. First, to reduce the prospects of a Gulf state's closer ties with the Soviet Union.[13] One reason that prompted the US to reflag 11 Kuwaiti tankers was the latter's agreement with the Soviet Union to charter three oil tankers. One of the major concerns of the US is how to deny the Soviet Union a premier patron's role in a region where western interests are relatively extensive. Preserving the dominant position of the West in the Gulf has required the US to beef-up the military capability of its regional allies. Second, to discourage any inclination of the Arab Gulf states to accommodate Iranian hegemony, the United States has attempted to make its security commitments more credible. Without the US support and security umbrella, these states would be vulnerable to Iranian intimidation. Recognising the intrinsically strategic character of the Gulf, the United States may not leave the region to the influence of a hostile power.[14] Third, enabling the Gulf states to defend their interests would support US and Western interests because they share a common interest in regional stability.

Among the Gulf states, Saudi Arabia has received large quantities of sophisticated US weapons. Saudi Arabia has bought F-15 jet fighters and has shown interest in obtaining the highly sophisticated C/D version of the F-16s which has been considered favourably by the US administration.[15] In 1987, US Defence Department approved the sale of 12 UH-60 troop carrying helicopters, 15 Bell 406s fitted as helicopter gunships with machine-guns and anti-tank rockets and C-12 Cargo planes. Also, the United States sold high tech radar jamming equipment for F-5 and F-15 jets.[16] But the US arms supply policy to its Middle East friends in the region has been influenced by the security concerns of Israel. Every sale has been assessed in terms of its impact on the Arab-Israeli military balance. Sale of certain type of weapons in the past has been blocked by the US Congress due to the opposition of the Pro-Israel lobby.[17] In such situations, Saudi Arabia and other Gulf states have turned to Britain, France and West Germany for the procurement of alternative weapon systems.

Sale of four Airborne Early Warning and Control Systems (AWACS) to Saudi Arabia is an important ingredient of regional support for the US military capabilities in the Gulf region. By agreement, US forces in the region share information gathered by the Saudi AWACS. In June 1987, the United States proposed to Saudi Arabia to extend joint air surveillance of shipping to the lower half of the Gulf.[18] The extension of this system southward would allow the United States to track the movement of all ships as they enter the Gulf. It would also provide escorting US warships early warning of any Iranian attack by motorboats, helicopters or one of the land-based Silkworm missiles. Also, weapons systems purchased by Saudi Arabia might be used by the US forces in emergencies which they would resupply later. Transferring some weapons to Saudi Arabia in excess might be considered a substitute for prepositioning equipment in the region.[19] Bahrain, Oman and the United Arab Emirates have also enhanced their military capabilities since the beginning of the Iran-Iraq War. The US stepped up weapons reinforcements of the Arab Gulf states between 1979-83 in addition to providing military training and constructing military facilities.[20] In return, Gulf states have extended quiet but varied cooperation which has significantly contributed to bolstering the US military presence.

Despite accelerated procurement of weapons and coordination of their diplomatic and security policies, the Arab Gulf countries may not be able to defend themselves effectively against a variety of threats. Foreign inspired subversion, internal dissent, and attacks against their shipping and oil installations constitute major threats to their security. Arab countries of the Gulf are so dependent on food imports and petro-dollars that their failure to defend against attacks on their shipping could have a devastating impact on their economies.[21] While some of the threats, such as internal subversion and political dissent may be met by greater coordination among the intelligence agencies, attacks on oil installations and shipping would require a US security umbrella. Only Saudi Arabia with AWACS, F-15 jet fighters, and other advanced equipment has developed enough capability to defend itself against the Iranian Air Force which due to the lack of spare parts has not maintained itself fully in a combat readiness position.

Limitations and Risks

The US interventionist strategy for the Gulf region has some serious limitations. Firstly, the task of getting enough forces with sufficient equipment to the conflict zone on time would be a hazardous operation. On paper, plans and numbers look pretty promising but under the impact of a real conflict situation in a distant area they may not work without sufficient cooperation of local allies. Despite significant reinforcement of strategic airlift capabilities, a protracted conflict would require the US much better mobility and logistics than are presently available.[22] Distance and geography pose another set of obstacles. Measures, such as keeping sufficient military equipment afloat near the Gulf, prepositioning of equipment at Diego Garcia, and acquisition of staging facilities in friendly states only partly resolve the dilemma posed by local geography and the distances involved between the United States and the Gulf military theatre. The support bases hitherto acquired by the United States are neither enough nor close to the likely theatres of conflict in the Persian Gulf. For effective operations, the US forces would need access to airfields and military facilities near the highest-threat area.[23]

The Arab states in the Gulf region which for various reasons qualify for US protection are reluctant to allow presence of American forces on their territory.[24] In an environment of anti-American sentiments, which has largely been shaped by pro-Israel US policies, it is extremely difficult for the rulers of these states to commit themselves too closely to the US military strategy in South West Asia. Although they are pretty autocratic in their policies, they have shown greater sensitivity to the public sentiment on the nature of their relationship with the United States. Despite the fact that the Gulf is a separate military theatre, its security issues cannot be isolated from Arab-Israeli affairs. The United States is generally seen as an ally of Israel. With the revolution in Iran, Islamic fundamentalists there and in other Muslim countries have extensively depicted the US as a power hostile to the interests of the Muslim world. A latent resentment against US Middle East policies has accumulated gradually among the Muslims in the Gulf and the Middle East. Their factor discourages the conservative rulers of Saudi Arabia and Gulf Shiekhdoms to identify themselves closely with the United States. To reduce political disability of friendly Arab regimes, the United States would have to develop rapport with the Muslim world, which looks unlikely unless the question of Palestine is amicably settled or the US distances itself from Israeli aggressiveness. Another factor is that, in recent years, Arab Gulf countries have not only attempted to make their nonaligned posture more credible but have also sought to balance their relations with the West. These states have increasingly realised that giving extensive access to US military power in the region would rather increase Soviet furtiveness to counterbalance the American military posture. On the other hand, keeping their security connections with the US limited and open to the Soviet diplomatic overtures would increase their flexibility.

Given the structure and doctrine of US forces, they are capable, and apparently willing to offer security assistance to the Gulf states against overt threats from Iran. Financing of Iraq's war efforts through long-term credits is one reason that has provoked Iran's hostility toward the GCC countries.[25] But their failure to assist Iraq could produce devastating strategic consequences. Under the turmoil, which might have followed the Iraqi defeat, at least the survival of pro-west regimes would have been problematic. At present Iraq's defeat appears the most unlikely outcome of the war. Firstly, the existing balance of capabilities between Iran and Iraq suggests that Iran's pursuit of a dominant political and military status is unrealiseable in the foreseeable future. Secondly, neither the regional states nor the superpowers wish to see such a fundamental change in the power equilibrium in the Gulf with Islamic Iran's dominance. To avert such an eventuality, the United States has adopted a dual-track policy. Firstly, US diplomacy has focused on achieving a cease-fire in the Gulf war by initiating evolution of consensus on an arms embargo against the belligerent that refuses to accept the UN cease-fire resolution 598.[26] At the same time, the US has been firmly communicating to Iran that her grand geopolitical designs would be met, if necessary, by force. US diplomacy to help end the war with no clear winner or loser is compatible with, and supportive of the interests of the Gulf states. Secondly, the United States has reinforced and maintained adequate forces in the vicinity of the Gulf to discourage Iran from escalating the war to "neutral" Arab states. Also, the aim is to prevent Iran from threatening the US protected shipping, and keeping the Strait of Hormuz open to oil traffic. While stridently opposing Iran's military and revolutionary threat to the region, the United States has carefully avoided initiating broad hostilities against Iran. This is perhaps more for a strategic interest in re-establishing ties with Iran in future.[27]

Iran's location and potential to play a major role in the South West Asian region would continue to attract US interest, no matter what the political orientation of its leaders is. Iran run by anti-American leaders is no less important to the US than an Iran under pro-west moderates. In the present state of distrust, US policy is directed towards achieving apparently two contradictory goals. The first relates to containing Iran's revolutionary expansionism. The US and the West have considerable stakes in defending the status quo political and security order in the region. The second objective is to explore the possibility of rapprochement with Iran. Perhaps, the United States having a neutral position in the Iran-Iraq War might have strengthened the prospects of an early understanding with Iran. The US proclamations of "neutrality" are not credible any longer, since its tilt toward Iraq is too obvious. In forestalling Iraq's defeat, US assistance has been significant. It has extended intelligence cooperation and credits to Baghdad and has encouraged regional and European allies to help reinforce Iraq's war fighting capability. This policy runs counter to the objective of restoring normal ties with Iran.

The dilemma which the US and the west face in the Gulf is how to deny Islamic revolutionary Iran dominance in the region without pushing her under the influence of the Soviet Union.[28] There are three potential developments that might trigger not only US confrontation with Iran but also create opportunities for the Soviet Union. First, the US might be compelled to use force to defend Gulf states against a direct Iranian attack. Second, Iran's attempts to block the oil traffic through the Strait of Hormuz would involve US forces for keeping the waterway open. In order to paralyse Iran's threat potential, the US might launch pre-emptive air strikes against the Iranian air and naval bases. Third, Iran's attacks against reflagged Kuwaiti tankers or US Naval escorts would precipitate punitive military strikes against the Iranian targets. Direct engagement of the US forces against Iran might produce two equally unwelcome consequences. Firstly, US attacks against Iran would enhance the prospects of the Soviet Union's strategic understanding with Tehran. Although the Soviet Union shares with the west interest in restraining Iran,[29] its leaders would be tempted to extend political and diplomatic support in the event of US air or naval strikes against Iran. In its confrontation with the US, Iran would equally be tempted to exercise the Soviet military option. Any prospects of the development of an Iran-Soviet alliance, which would essentially be a marriage of convenience, might upset the US strategic planning in the region, and present the western alliance with difficult options.

Secondly, direct confrontation between the US and Iran might not be limited to a few exchanges. The US has the ability to launch and, perhaps, sustain punitive strikes against Iran, but it would face serious difficulties in protecting its forces fighting a defensive war in tiny Gulf states. That is, perhaps, the worst case scenario. But, even in less threatening situations, Iran has the capability to harass US forces in the Gulf. This would not require the involvement of large forces. The Iranian capability and pattern of naval war suggests that it would rely on planting mines. Iran has achieved the capability to manufacture better and more sophisticated mines that would make detection difficult. Secondly, Iran would use high speed missile boats against larger US naval targets. Armed with relatively small weapons, they may not sink a large vessel, but the success of their attacks would raise a morale problem for the US forces. Thirdly, acquisition of Chinese Silkworm missiles[30] fired from the Iranian coastline would be capable of sinking even larger vessels. Jihad inspired suicide missions would add altogether a new dimension. Needless to say, Americans are sensitive to criticism that the US is politically less capable of fighting a protracted war in the Gulf region.[31]

Whether the Kremlin constitutes a threat to the western interests in the Gulf region would depend on one's interpretation of the Soviet Union's intentions and capabilities. Having an overwhelming Asian geography, pursuing an active Third World diplomacy, and engaged in a competition with the United States, the Soviet interest in outflanking the western influence in the Gulf is quite natural. Therefore, denial of this region to the Soviet Union through military deterrence and diplomatic initiatives constitutes the major aim of US policy.

At present the US and the west do not seem to be facing a serious challenge from the Soviet Union. Firstly, the Gulf states have traditionally pursued pro-west policies and have shown serious apprehensions about Soviet intentions. With their military intervention in Afghanistan, the Soviets have further damaged their image and credibility.[32] Secondly, with the revolution in Iran and the Gulf war the Soviet Union has confronted serious difficulties in expanding her influence. Iran's leaders are equally hostile to the Soviet Union for its support to Iraq and intervention in Afghanistan. Even Iraq, a lone and long-time Soviet ally in the Gulf, has gradually turned to the US and pro-west monarchies for support in its war against Iran. As a result, Iraq has distanced itself from Moscow and has pursued a more balanced policy. The Soviet Union's relations with Kuwait, Oman and UAE have remained more or less ceremonial. It achieved some success with Kuwait first by selling a limited quantity of weapons and then leasing oil tankers. Chartering the Soviet tankers served more Kuwait's purpose of involving both the superpowers deeply in efforts to stop the Gulf war than producing any diplomatic coup for Moscow. It seems that the political and security environment of the region is not conducive to a major diplomatic or political change in favour of the Soviet Union. Thirdly, the Soviet Union has neither the resources nor is it willing to risk confrontation with the US by posing a military threat to western interests. Soviet leaders have carefully avoided challenging the western interests for two reasons. First, the US military capabilities in the region are quite formidable. The Soviet Union faced with diplomatic constraints in the region and resource problems is not currently capable of matching the US forces. Second, the fear of horizontal and vertical escalation of conflict with the United States would continue to discourage a direct Soviet military threat to the US interests.

Two factors, however, might assist the Soviet Union in its quest for gaining influence in the Gulf. First, the erosion of US credibility with its Arab allies. One reason that Kuwait turned to the Soviet Union for chartering oil tankers was the information that the US was secretly shipping weapons to Iran. Second, the marked decline in US economic power. Keeping the Soviets away from the Gulf would depend much on US ability, both political and economic, to stay in the region.

Threats to security which appear to be difficult to manage by any foreign interventionist force would be internal political upheavals. These might be caused by a wide range of factors. Among them, appeal of Islamic fundamentalism and internal power struggles might play important roles. The state and society on the Arab side of the Gulf have been undergoing rapid changes over the past fifteen years. Despite fundamental changes in the life style of masses in these societies, the traditional political structures have shown remarkable stability. The regimes and their leaders feel more self-assured and confident than a decade ago. Yet, potential for destabilisation does exist with vast disparities between life-styles and incomes of the ruling dynasties and the common man. In the past, satisfaction of material needs has kept the societies quiet and complacent. But for how long can economic satisfaction keep the mass political consciousness below the level of assertiveness for sharing political power? This is not to suggest that the traditional political culture of these societies lacks flexibility to accommodate political aspirations of new affluent classes that might seek political influence. Nor, does it mean that a political storm is brewing under the surface of political stability which would inevitably overtake the present political arrangements.

There are strong grounds to believe, however, that foreign assisted covert activities and local disaffection with the current family fiefdoms might promote political chaos that would threaten the control of ruling elites in the Arab Peninsula states. One must acknowledge the fact that effective attainment of US and western economic and security interests in the southwest Asian region would highly depend not only on the credible deterrence of the US forces in the Gulf but also on the stable and effective control of the ruling families in the Gulf states. If the political orientation of revolutionary Iran is any guide, any radical group that topples pro-west dynasties in the Arab Gulf states, by political necessity, would be hostile to US and western interests. President Reagan's assertion that "we will not allow Saudi Arabia to become another Iran"[33] underscores the importance of stable control of the dynastic elites in the Gulf states. But beyond indirect support, what makes such an assertion unrealistic is that US forces are neither designed nor capable of ensuring a regime's survival in the face of a popular revolutionary movement.

Another factor that complicates Washington's Gulf strategy is its allies' (Western Europe, Japan) refusal to commit their forces in support of US military tasks in the Persian Gulf. This is despite the fact that they are more dependent on Gulf oil than the United States.[34] Independently, Britain and France have deployed large naval forces, but they seem reluctant to build-up a war fighting capability in concert with the US.[35] However, should the situation worsen, we might see a greater coordinated response from the members of the western alliance.[36]

Conclusion

US Indian Ocean strategy is essentially Gulf-centred, and is aimed at achieving a military capability for a direct involvement in Gulf security contingencies. Western interests in oil and markets, and developments since the revolution in Iran, have greatly influenced US measures to strengthen its power projection capabilities to the South West Asian region. This policy is premised on the assumption that given the complex threat environment, the protection of Western interests would largely depend on US military deterrence. Capability to initiate and sustain asymmetrical responses to a variety of threats is the central component of US military deterrence in the region.

Strengthening of the US military capabilities in the region has involved three main actions. First, the United States has significantly increased its military presence in the Gulf, which is supported by an aircraft carrier battle group deployed in the Arabian Sea. Second, US strategic planning for the Gulf has focused on increasing the rapid deployment capability of its forces. To support their mobility and military action, the United States has secured access to a variety of local facilities. Third, the defence capabilities of pro-west states in the region have been strengthened through transfer of appropriate and advanced military equipment. Low-profile and informal military cooperation with the United States has helped the Arab Gulf countries achieve a greater measure of security. A tacit division of labour seems to have evolved between the US and the GCC to defend their common interests. GCC countries would enhance cooperation among themselves to deal with internal subversion and political unrest, while the US would establish a protective presence in the vicinity to prevent external intervention.

US security policy is aimed at ensuring that the Gulf region is not destabilised by revolutionary Iran or the Soviet Union. The Soviet Union lacks the capability to challenge western dominance in the region. Regional political constraints and threat of horizontal and vertical escalation would sufficiently dissuade the Soviet leaders from risking confrontation with the US in the Gulf. Iran's revolutionary expansionism and its quest to restructure the political and security order of the region presents rather a serious dilemma to the United States. While striving to contain Iran, the United States would like to carefully avoid military conflict with Iran. Confrontation with Iran would not only diminish further the possibility of re-establishing normal ties but might also push Iran toward Moscow.

NOTES

1. President Carter outlined this policy in his State of the Union address (January 1980) **Public Papers of the Presidents. Jimmy Carter,** 1980-81, pp.196-7.
2. Weinberger, **Department of Defense Annual Report, Fiscal Year 1984,** (Washington: GPO, 1 February 1983), p.37.
3. "What Next in the Gulf?" **International Herald Tribune,** 22 June 1987, p.4; **International Herald Tribune,** 1 June 1987, p.1, 2.
4. See a memorandum prepared in the Office of the Assistant Secretary of Defence (Program Analysis and Evaluation), "Capabilities in the Persian Gulf," 15 June 1979.
5. Ibid., p.2.
6. William Stivers, **America's Confrontation with Revolutionary Change in the Middle East, 1948-83** (London: Macmillan Press, 1986), p.87.
7. House subcommittee on Europe and the Middle East, **Persian Gulf 1980,** pp.94-5; House Committee on the Budget, **Rapid Deployment Joint Task Forces,** 45-7; Congressional Reference Service, **Rapid Deployment Force,** p.12; Congressional Reference Service, **Defence Budget FY 1983; Strategic Mobility** (Airlift and Sealift); Issue Brief Number 1B82035, 10 September 1982.
8. US, Congress, Congressional Budget Office, **Rapid Deployment Forces: Policy and Budgetary Implications**, February 1983, p.XV; **New York Times,** 25 October 1982, pp.A1, A14.
9. Thomas L. McNaugher, "Balancing Soviet Power in the Persian Gulf," **The Brookings Review,** (Summer 1983), p.22.
10. Harold Brown, **Department of Defence Annual Report, Fiscal Year 1981**, pp.11, 209-14.
11. Ibid.
12. US, Congress, House subcommittee on Military Construction Appropriations, Committee on Appropriations, **Military Construction Appropriation for 1981**, 96th Congress, 2nd

session, p.1061; **Washington Post,** 7 August 1980, p.Al.

13. Richard W. Murphy, **"International Shipping and the Iran-Iraq War"** current policy No. 958 (Washington, D.C., Dept. of State, May 1987) p.3. See also, "Pentagon Reportedly Beefs Up Role in Gulf" **Congressional Quarterly**, August, 1987, p.1740.
14. "The Right Note on the Gulf" **International Herald Tribune**, 18 June 1987, p.4.
15. **Frontier Post** (Peshawar), 29 January 1987.
16. **Nation** (Lahore), 29 March 1987.
17. President Reagan withdrew the proposal to sell 1600 Maverick anti-tank missiles after 67 Senators backed a resolution blocking the sale. **International Herald Tribune**, 21-22 June 1987, p.2.
18. **Muslim** (Islamabad), 8 June 1987.
19. McNaugher, p.23.
20. **Frontier Post**, January, 1987.
21. See Robert G. Neuman and Shireen T. Hunter, "Crisis in the Gulf: Reasons for concern But not for panic" **American Arab Affairs**, No. 9, (Summer 1984), p.19; **International Herald Tribune**, 6-7 June 1987.
22. See opinion of General John A. Wickham Jr., **International Herald Tribune**, 18 June 1987.
23. Statement of Chairman of the Joint Chiefs of Staff Admiral William J. Crowe Jr. **International Herald Tribune**, 1 June 1987, p.5.
24. For instance see a statement of UAE's Petroleum and Mineral Resources Minister Dr. Mana Saeed Al Otaiba, **Muslim**, 15 June 1987.
25. Until April 1984, Saudi Arabia alone provided $25 Billion to Iraq. **South**, November 1987, p.49.
26. United Nations security council unanimously passed resolution 598 in July 1987, which is mandatory in nature. The Soviet Union and the United States have been consulting each other on stopping the Gulf war and giving some substance to the proposal for an arms embargo against Iran.

See an interview of Yuli M. Vorontsov, **International Herald Tribune**, 8 June 1987; **Frontier Post**, 10 May 1987.

27. See, Stansfield Turner, "The Gulf: A Tough Beat For America to Police," **International Herald Tribune**, 2 June 1987.

28. On this argument see, Barry Rubin, "Drowning in the Gulf" **Foreign Policy** No. 69. (Winter 1987/88), p.121.

29. "Gulf: Parallel Courses" **International Herald Tribune**, 14 May 1987; see also David Hirst, "The explosive twist in Gulf War," **Frontier Post**, 24 March 1987.

30. **New York Times**, 15 March 1987, pp.1,16.

31. Robert J. Hanks (Rear Admiral Ret.), "The Gulf War and U.S. Staying Power," **Strategic Review** (Fall 1987), pp.36-43.

32. Karen Dawisha, "Moscow's Moves in the Direction of the Gulf-So Near and Yet So Far," **Journal Of International Affairs**, Vol. 34, No. 2 (Fall/Winter 1980/81), p.220.

33. Cited by Michael Sterner, "Perceptions and Policies of the Gulf States Towards Regional Security and the Superpower Rivalry" in (ed.) Alvin Z. Rubinstein, **The Great Game: Rivalry in the Persian Gulf and South Asia** (New York: Praeger 1983), p.39.

34. Only 7 percent of US oil needs come from the Gulf whereas the region supplies 70 percent of Japan's oil needs and half the requirements of Western Europe. See **Dawn**, 5 May 1987.

35. Edward Cody, "Allies Cool to US Call for Joint Effort in Gulf," **International Herald Tribune**, 1 June 1987; "US and the Gulf," **Nation**, 8 June 1987, Lou Cannon, "Reagan Receives Tepid Support on Terror, Gulf" **International Herald Tribune**, 20 June 1987, pp.1, 7; Lord Carrington the NATO Secretary General also opposed NATO action in the Gulf. **Muslim**, 1 June 1987.

36. For a similar view see, Claude Rakisits, **The Gulf Conflict: Recent Developments and International Implications**, current issues paper 10 (Canberra: Legislative Research Service, Department of the Parliamentary Library, 1988), pp.21-30.

Comments

Mohammed Ayoob

The importance of the Gulf in any discussion of the Indian Ocean region is obvious. It is that sub-region of the Indian Ocean region which is not only most prone to instability and conflict, it has had a major war raging within it for the past eight years. More than the actual conflict between Iran and Iraq that goes on in the Gulf, the Iranian revolution, as Rais has pointed out more than once in his paper, has unleashed a process for which the West, in particular the United States, has still to find an adequate response. As he has very ably argued in his paper, the American response to the changes in the Gulf brought about by the Iranian revolution and its aftermath have been military, although the challenges that the Iranian revolution posed to American hegemony in the Gulf and to the power hierarchy in the international order were primarily political and ideological in character. A military response to what is primarily a political challenge is more often than not counter-productive because it does not respond to, and cannot really respond to, the major ingredient of such a challenge which in the case of the Iranian revolution, and the ideology that the revolution preached and tried to operationalize in political terms, was that the people of Iran, and of the Gulf, indeed of the entire Third World had the right to decide their own fate. It was an ideology which emphasized autonomy—the autonomy to decide one's fate—and one cannot respond to the urge to become the master of one's own destiny by deploying the Rapid Deployment Force, by establishing the Central Command, or by deploying carrier battle groups, in and around the Gulf.

These might be retaliatory measures and they might be able to temporarily contain the revolutionary contagion, but there are no long term military solutions to such a phenomenon. I am very glad that Rais did bring this conclusion out very forthrightly. Irrespective of what one thinks of the Iranian revolution or those who rule Iran today, the major thrust of the Iranian revolution was toward achieving national autonomy, and I think it would be misunderstanding the essence of that revolution and the demonstration effect of that even on the Gulf sub-region if one gets carried away by writings in popular magazines which brand Ayatollah Khomeini and his colleagues as "mad mullahs" who threaten Western civilization.

As I have stated earlier, the problem that the Iranian revolution posed for global order was that it challenged the way the power hierarchy in the international system was organized. It is very instructive in this context to analyze the policies of the great powers towards the Iran-Iraq war. It is very interesting to note that while on the one hand the Americans extend large amounts of credit to Iraq and indulge in minesweeping and oil-tanker reflagging operations which are all clearly directed against Iran, at the same time the French supply state-of-the art armour to Iraq. This is a very interesting congruence or coincidence of the interests of all major external powers whether western or eastern, as far as the Iran-Iraq conflict is concerned. This coincidence of interests arises out of the fact that the Iranian challenge transcends American-Iranian relations; it is not merely a challenge to the United States, it is as much, if not more, a challenge to the Soviet Union and of course, to America's European allies. This is why you see this collective tilt of all major powers towards Iraq.

This pattern is duplicated at the regional level as well because Iran's revolution was also a challenge to the established regional order in the Gulf. The Iraqi invasion of Iran was the regional establishment's military response to the political and ideological challenge posed by Iran just as the RDF, the Centcom, and the deployment of the carrier battle groups were the global system's military response to the political and ideological challenge that the revolution posed. Iran's regional opponents included Saudi Arabia and the smaller Gulf monarchies. While they had no particular love for the Iraqi regime they bank-rolled its war effort to the tune of tens of billions of dollars. These monarchies who are allied to the United States, if not formally at least informally, found it convenient to support Iraq which was getting most of its arms at that stage from the Soviet Union and, in fact, had signed a Treaty of Peace, Friendship and Cooperation with the Soviet Union. They did so because they fully realized that the threat the revolution posed was to all of them, whether allied to the Soviet Union or the United States, and whether secular or religious in terms of their regime's distinguishing characteristics.

The Iranian Revolution and the Iran-Iraq war have also had implications, as Rais has pointed out, for the Arab-Israeli conflict, particularly in terms of American policy. The American capacity to meet the Iranian challenge has been reduced because of the suspicions harboured even by America's strongest Arab allies regarding American policies towards the Arab-Israeli issue which they see as endorsing Israeli occupation of Arab territories. However, there is also a connection between the Gulf and the region to its east, namely South Asia. After all Iran, at one time after the Indo-Pakistan war of 1971, had tried to act as the guarantor of Pakistan's territorial integrity and the Shah had put in a massive effort in supporting the Pakistani regime after that war. Recently the purchase by Saudi Arabia of IRBMs from China has led to apprehensions among strategic analysts in India that there could be a use that these IRBMs could be put to in relation to India itself because there is a very close military relationship between Pakistan and Saudi Arabia. Until recently 20,000 Pakistani soldiers served in Saudi Arabia and the Saudis have also been bank-rolling the Pakistani purchases of various types of sophisticated military equipment including the F-16 aircraft. There has been speculation in India whether these IRBMs may not at some stage be moved to the sub-continent and may become a factor that would have to be taken into account in terms of the evolving nuclear equation between India and Pakistan.

If the Gulf is important in global terms because of its oil, its strategic location, etc., it is also very important for the two contiguous regions, the Arab heartland on the one hand and South Asia on the other. So far, not enough thought has been given to these inter-region connections around the Indian Ocean littoral and the effects on them of the Iran-Iraq war and the consequent inflow of very sophisticated military hardware into the Gulf.

CHAPTER 6

Australia and the Persian Gulf Conflict: The Public Perception of the War*

Claude G.P. Rakisits

Australia and the Persian Gulf Conflict

A. Introduction

Australia's interest in the seven-and-a-half-year-old Persian Gulf conflict has been limited, at best, and non-existent, at worse. Most people would probably say that this is to be expected since that area of the world is a long way away from our shores and, therefore, not of direct strategic interest to Australia. However, when examining in greater detail the Persian Gulf and its relationship with Australia, one will soon conclude that the lack of public interest in the region's developments is quite misplaced and could, potentially, be of great detriment to our national interests.

Australia's interest in the events of the Gulf should be guided by two main factors: our trade inks with the countries of the area and the effect the on-going conflict may have on our Western allies' economic well-being. In the area of trade, Australia is essentially concerned with assuring that our oil supply is not threatened or interrupted and that our export markets remain safe from external or internal disruptions. Secondly, as full-fledged

* The views expressed in this paper are the author's. They may not necessarily be the same as the department's.

members of the Western alliance we have a political, military and economic interest to ensure that the Persian Gulf conflict does not threaten our allies' economic interests. As a minimum, it is in our economic self-interest that our allies' economic position remain stable and free from any possible disruption of oil supply from the Persian Gulf, since they are an essential export market for our goods and commodities. Consequently, while Australia has no direct strategic interest in the Persian Gulf, it is in Australia's national interest to ensure, within its limited capabilities, that there are no political and military developments in the region which could ultimately be detrimental to our economic stability.

B. Australia's Trade Interests

For the last fifteen years the Persian Gulf has become increasingly important to the Australian economy as a market for its primary produce, manufactured goods and services. In 1986, the Persian Gulf area had become Australia's fifth largest export market and it ranked eighth on our list of suppliers, mainly as our major source of imported oil.

As Table 1 indicates, Australian trade with the Persian Gulf countries has continued to increase since 1980, in spite of the fact that two of the major countries in the area have been at war with one another. However, while in 1986 the total amount of Australian exports to the region amounted to a 57 per cent increase over the 1980 period, Australia's imports took an opposite direction; we witnessed a drop of 48 per cent in total imports over the same period.[1] In absolute terms this meant a drop of approximately $400 million in the total volume of trade between Australia and the Gulf States in the last six years. Because of this drop in the Gulf's exports, Australia managed to reverse quite dramatically in our favour the trade imbalance which had been present since the 1970s. This was mainly as a result of not only Iran's and Iraq's substantial drop in export to Australia, but also due to diminished Australian imports from all other Gulf states, except Oman and Qatar which increased their exports to Australia. This resulted in Australia improving its trading position with all Persian Gulf states, except with Qatar.

The region has been the leading market for live animals, cheese and curd and barley, with Saudi Arabia being the main destination for these exports. The Gulf is also a major market for

TABLE 1

AUSTRALIAN TRADE WITH THE GULF STATES
($'000)

Country	Australia's Exports	Australia's Imports	Australia's Excess Of Exports
BAHRAIN			
(1980/81)	56,176	109,848	- 53,672
(1986)	80,016	35,222	+ 44,794
IRAN			
(1980/81)	196,471	33,418	+ 163,053
(1986)	383,564	4,059	+ 379,505
IRAQ			
(1980/81)	59,265	95,738	- 36,473
(1986)	197,033	95	+ 196,938
KUWAIT			
(1980/81)	182,539	350,768	- 168,229
(1986)	109,480	187,563	- 78,083
OMAN			
(1980/81)	25,752	NIL	+ 25,752
(1986)	53,627	15,463	+ 38,164
QATAR			
(1980/81)	15,776	232	+ 15,544
(1986)	29,755	76,124	- 46,369
SAUDI ARABIA			
(1980/81)	276,305	1,022,604	- 746,299
(1986)	393,393	421,744	- 28,351
UNITED ARAB EMIRATES			
(1980/81)	103,167	195,245	- 92,078
(1986)	199,324	130,781	+ 68,543
TOTAL			
(1980/81)	915,451	1,807,853	- 892,402
(1986)	1,446,192	871,051	+ 575,141

* Source: Composition of Trade, Department of Trade, 1986.

the sale of wheat (Iran and Iraq) and mutton and lamb (United Arab Emirates, Iran and Saudi Arabia). Incidentally, Australia's $80 million live sheep trade with Saudi Arabia might well be in jeopardy if local producers fail to meet strict export requirements. In a move to increase the quality of meat consumed in Saudi Arabia, the Saudi government has recently restricted live sheep imports to sheep under three years old; and by August next year the maximum age limit will be two years old. According to the director of the Sheepmeat Council of Australia, it was unlikely that the industry would be able to meet these new requirements.[2]

As expected, our imports from that region is mainly composed of crude petroleum oils and refined petroleum products; and the amount we import is certainly not insignificant. In 1986 we needed to import approximately 20 per cent of our total oil need, 66.5 per cent of which came from the Persian Gulf. This meant that about 15 per cent of Australia's total crude oil needs was imported from that region, with 45 per cent coming from Saudi Arabia alone.[3] This figure goes up to approximately 19 per cent if one includes the refined petroleum products which are imported from Singapore but which are essentially refined Saudi crude. While 15 to 19 per cent may not seem as much, it is the fact that most of this imported oil is heavy crude—the basic oil type for industry—which gives this figure greater significance.[4] Consequently, a prolonged interruption of oil supply from the Persian Gulf, and especially from Saudi Arabia, would be highly disruptive to the Australian economy.

However, on a more optimistic note, a closure of the Strait of Hormuz would not necessarily create as much disruption as one would generally imagine. Since 1980 Saudi Arabia and Iraq, in a clear attempt to avoid having to be totally dependent on the freedom of navigation through the Strait of Hormuz to export their oil, decided to build a number of overland pipelines across Saudi Arabia and Turkey. The result has been that in the period from 1980 until 1987 the amount of oil which has to go through the Strait has been reduced from 92 per cent of total export down to only 63 per cent. Put differently, in 1980 31 per cent of total Persian Gulf export to the OECD countries went through the Strait; this was reduced to 17 per cent by 1987.[5] Unfortunately, it was not possible to determine how much of our oil imports from the Persian Gulf goes through the Strait. Presumably, the majority does, since it is the shortest route between the Gulf and

Australia.

Briefly, Australia has sought to establish closer formal relations with the region by signing a number of Trade, Economic and Technical Cooperation Agreements with the countries of the area. Accordingly, Australia had concluded such agreements with: Bahrain (1979), Iraq (1980), Saudi Arabia (1980), Oman (1981), Kuwait (1982) and the United Arab Emirates (1985). Australia is presently negotiating with Iran a new trade agreement which would supersede the one which was signed in 1974. Complementing these agreements are the Joint Commissions we have with Saudi Arabia and Iraq. There is a possibility that another one will be established with Iran in the near future.

Unfortunately, while on the one hand Australia has gradually increased the number of formal trade agreements it has entered into with Persian Gulf countries, it has on the other hand reduced the number of diplomatic and trade commissioner (now Austrade) posts in the area. By the late 1970s Australia had Trade Commissioner posts in: Abu Dhabi, Baghdad, Bahrain, Jeddah, Kuwait and Tehran. However, by 1986, Australia had withdrawn most of these posts and only had Austrade representatives in Dubai in the United Arab Emirates and in Jeddah and Riyadh in Saudi Arabia. Moreover, it had also closed down our embassies in Bahrain and Kuwait and the consulate-general in Abu Dhabi, reducing our presence in the region to Iran, Iraq and Saudi Arabia.

C. Australia's Strategic Interests

The Persian Gulf is of no direct military strategic interest to Australia, since the north-wet Indian Ocean is well beyond the area of Australia's primary strategic interest. As stated in the government's March 1987 Defence Policy Information Paper, the government's emphasis in the defence planning of the country is on developments in South-east Asia and the South-West Pacific, where there are substantial and increasing calls on the Australian Defence Force's resources. However, this does not mean that Australia does not have a common concern with other non-Communist industrialised countries to secure a continued supply of oil from the Persian Gulf. It is in Australia's strategic and economic interest to ensure that its Western and Japanese trade partners remain economically stable to enable the continued export of Australian goods and services to these countries.

Consequently, it is because the Persian Gulf is such a key strategic region of the world—providing approximately 30 per cent and 60 per cent of Western Europe's and Japan's oil needs, respectively; being connected to the Indian Ocean; and being relatively close to the Soviet Union and Afghanistan—that it is in Australia's interest to ensure that the present instability in the region does not escalate into a major conflict which would involve direct active military participation by outside powers, particularly the superpowers.

Already back in 1977, the members of the Joint Committee on Foreign Affairs and Defence of the Australian Parliament did not underestimate the potential for instability, and the possible consequences it could have for Australia, if a conflict developed in the Middle East. In their final Report the Committee observed as follows:

> Should the worst happen and a Middle East conflict escalate beyond the region the US—Australia's ally—would be likely to be involved. Even in a localised war, heavy diplomatic and military resource demands are made on the US. Increases in tension in the regions such as the Middle East, where the superpowers' strategic interests are great and where their policies are interwoven and may conflict, tend to increase Australia's own strategic uncertainty and insecurity. Therefore it is in Australia's interests to foster peace and stability in the Middle East region; this can best be achieved by good offices, through encouragement so that military action would be less likely to be contemplated.[6]

The above recommendation, while more than ten years old, has essentially been the Australian government's position vis-a-vis the Persian Gulf conflict. Being only a middle-ranking country, Australia has had to limit its efforts to the diplomatic sphere in an attempt to safeguard its economic and national interests in the region. Accordingly, the government has been most active at the United Nations. However, this does not mean that it has not provided, or been willing to provide, direct and indirect military assistance to its Western allies, particularly the United States.

D. Australian Government Policy

Since the beginning of the hostilities Australia has endeavoured to maintain an even-handed approach in its dealings with both participants, and has on numerous occasions called on both Iran and Iraq to agree on a cease-fire and begin peace negotiations. The Australian Government has made this position quite clear on several occasions, including in Prime Minister Hawke's report to Parliament on his January 1987 visit to the Middle-East. However, the Australian Government's "position of strict neutrality" does not mean that it has not been concerned with the human cost of the war.[7] For example, Australia has on three occasions provided an expert, Dr. Peter Dunn, to play a leading role in the United Nations Secretary General's investigating team examining Iraq's alleged use of chemical weapons in the present conflict. Foreign Minister Hayden declared on 31 March 1985

> The Government has always stated in vehement terms its abhorrence of chemical weapons. The latest allegations underline the importance of concluding a comprehensive convention to outlaw chemical weapons and the need for effective verification provisions. The Government would do all it could to facilitate the early conclusion of such a convention and the strengthening of the role of the United Nations Secretary General in investigating allegations of the use of chemical weapons.[8]

In addition, when Australia was a member of the UN Security Council in 1985 and 1986 it strongly supported Resolution 582 which deplored the initial acts which gave rise to the conflict as well as the continuation of the conflict. Accordingly, in a news release on 25 February 1986, Foreign Minister Hayden welcomed the unanimous adoption of this resolution. Similarly, the Australian Government also welcomed the passage of UN Security Council Resolution 598 which demands an immediate cease-fire and withdrawal of all forces to internationally recognised boundaries. Answering a question asked on 23 September 1987 by the leader of the Opposition, Mr John Howard, Prime Minister Hawke re-affirmed Australia's support for Resolution 598.

> This Government will continue to work for effective action in the United Nations on the basis of Security

> Council Resolution 598 which, we believe, provides an honourable and proper basis for negotiations to end this dispute. We will continue to press within the United Nations for action along those lines and, specifically, we believe appropriate that there should be an embargo on the provision of arms to Iran as the Leader of the Opposition suggested.[9]

The Australian Government's position on this issue has bi-partisan support, since Mr Howard then declared that "the Opposition strongly associates itself with what the Prime Minister has said."[10]

The Australian Government has always shown its preference for a United-Nations-directed resolution to the conflict rather than through direct superpower involvement. For example, while the Minister for Foreign Affairs and Trade, Mr Hayden, stated that "it was a matter of deep regret that the U.S.-registered vessel *Bridgeton* has struck a mine during its voyage to Kuwait" and "re-affirmed Australia's deep commitment to the right of freedom of navigation", he reiterated that "Australia has consistently supported the responsibility of the Security Council for the maintenance of international peace and security."[11]

However, within two months, when it became obvious that the United Nations Security Council Resolution 598 would probably never be implemented, the Australian Government had shifted its attitude towards outside involvement in the conflict, accepting instead selective direct United States military action against Iran. For example, the Australian Government strongly supported United States action against Iranian targets following the latter's military action attacks against Kuwait and laying of mines in the Gulf. The Acting Minister for Foreign Affairs and Trade, Senator Gareth Evans, declared, after the United States took military action against Iranian patrol boats reportedly laying mines, that

> The United States along with other Western nations had been forthrightly attempting to preserve the right of freedom of navigation in the Persian Gulf...The Australian Government believed the United States had acted fully within its inherent right of self-defence as it was broadly entitled under Article 51 of the Charter of the United-Nations.[12]

The Minister for Foreign Affairs and Trade, Mr Hayden,

re-affirmed this support for US military action against offensive Iranian military activity when he stated on 20 October 1987 that the United States' destruction of an Iranian oil platform as a response to Tehran's missile attack on the US-flagged *Sea Isle City* "was conducted within its inherent right of self-defence ...and represented a proportionate response to an ongoing threat to American vessels and crews."[13]

The Australian Government's justified concern for neutral shipping in the Gulf was dramatically borne out following the unprovoked Iraqi attack, on 1 October, 1987, against the *Shenton Bluff* flying the Australian flag in international waters. Declaring that this action was in clear breach of international law, Mr Hayden stated that the Australian Government "condemned and protested in the strongest possible terms."[14]

As previously indicated, Australia has also contributed indirectly to the protection of civilian shipping in the Persian Gulf by granting the United States military facilities. Three important elements in this military contribution have been the hosting of a naval communication facility at North West Cape, granting US Navy usage of Fremantle and Cockburn Sound for port visits, and allowing US B52 bombers transit rights at Darwin airport. These port and defence facilities allow aircraft and satellite surveillance and intelligence gathering, support for naval (including submarine) communications and signals, monitoring of general naval activity and ensure ease of communications between the Pacific and the area of vital interest to the United States in the North-Western Indian Ocean.[15]

Australia also demonstrated its credentials as a reliable member of the Western Alliance when, in the wake of the Soviet invasion of Afghanistan and the increased tensions in the Persian Gulf, it sent the aircraft carrier HMAS *Melbourne* and escort vessels to the Indian Ocean at the end of 1980.

More recently, and certainly of greater relevance to present developments in the Persian Gulf, the Australian Government examined various options for contributing to the security of shipping using the Persian Gulf. In a Cabinet submission, which was 'leaked' to **The Sydney Morning Herald** and published on 27 November 1987, it was revealed that the US had informally approached the Australian Government, suggesting that Australia go beyond mere rhetorical support and, instead, participate militarily in the protection of international shipping in the Gulf. In the submission, the Minister for Defence, Mr Kim Beazley, suggested three options which the Australian Government could consider in case Washington made a formal request for Australian participation. These options were: first, a Clearance Diving Team comprising 20 personnel, trained to clear ships' hulls of explosive attachments and to disarm mines to a depth of 52 metres; second, a RAAF Orion maritime surveillance aircraft to be deployed in Diego Garcia in the Indian Ocean or Oman to operate in the region; and, third, sending an Australian Navy FFG frigate to the Gulf. Reportedly, Mr Beazley's favoured option was the Clearance Diving Team; since it would be clearly defensive in nature, integrated with the US (or perhaps UK) forces or based ashore and it would be the least expensive of all three options. He recommended that, if this option were implemented, its initial period should be for a period of no longer than one year. The Orion aircraft option was seen as not only inappropriate for the present situation, given that this aircraft is primarily designed for anti-submarine warfare, but also a commitment which would seriously affect Australia's survelliance capability in South-East Asia and the South Pacific. Finally, sending a frigate would be more likely than the other options to draw Australia into any escalation of hostilities. Moreover, it was thought that it might contribute to the already high level of tension and, certainly, would be the most expensive of the three options.

Eventually, the Australian Government decided on 10 December 1987 to make available a Clearance Diving Team from the RAN to assist in the operations "that are helping to maintain freedom of navigation in the Persian Gulf."[16] Mr Beazley declared that

> The deployment of a clearance diving team is appropriate to the mining threat in the Gulf and wholly defensive in nature...Our assistance will directly support the safety of shipping in the Gulf and our commitment to freedom of navigation.[17]

Pointing out that Australia had substantial trade with the Persian Gulf countries, the Minister for Defence added that

> As a major trading nation Australia has a clear national interest in upholding the principle of supporting safe civilian shipping and of freedom of

> navigation on international waterways... In all, some 330 Australian and foreign flag ships were involved in carrying Australian cargo in the Gulf in the first ten months of 1987.[18]

Accordingly, he justified Australian military participation on the basis that

> The Government is of the view that it would be inappropriate for Australia to benefit from the efforts made by friendly countries to keep open the Gulf shipping routes without making a substantial effort of our own, within the limits of our capacity to do so, and bearing in mind the need to ensure the safety of the personnel involved.[19]

However, in anticipation of a possible formal American request for Australian participation in the protection of shipping in the Gulf, the Australian Government decided to have the diving team attached to a Royal Navy ship involved directly in protecting Australian flagships and Australian cargo carried in vessels flying the flags of other nations instead of a US ship. Moreover, the team would be under Australian command. By choosing to have this diving team attached to a British ship the Hawke Government avoided the possibility of being placed in the awkward position of having to balance its "moral" obligation as a member of the Western alliance and its domestic need to reassure the Australian public and the left wing of the Australian Labor Party that Australian participation did not necessarily mean the beginning of an open-ended Vietnam-type military commitment. Moreover, by attaching itself to the Royal Navy it reflected a shift in emphasis away from the Government's wish to "prove" its credentials as a loyal ally of the US to one of making a direct contribution to the protection of Australian trade passing through the Persian Gulf. Finally, Mr Beazley argued that it was doubtful that Iran would retaliate economically against Australia if we did send a diving team to the Gulf. He pointed out that Iran had not taken such measures against other countries which had already taken part in military action in the region, and all of them traded more with Iran than Australia did.[20] However, all these guarantees were ineffective in reassuring the Australian Democrats, the left wing of the Labor Party and certain sections of the media, that this "symbolic" military contribution was not going to lead to Australia getting involved in a far-away military conflict.

E. Reaction to Possible Australian Involvement

Basically, the whole debate about whether or not Australia should send a Clearance Diving Team to the Persian Gulf has become relatively academic. Although the divers are standing by, ready to be dispatched to the Gulf on short notice, it is now almost certain that the Australian government will not be sending the team to the Gulf. This is in view of the fact that not only have the western minesweepers from the US, Britain, France, Italy, Belgium and the Netherlands not found any mines for months, but since the *Bridgeton* struck a mine in July 1987 not a single oil tanker has run into a mine. The danger of hitting a mine seems to have receded to such an extent that the Western participants are now looking for ways to cut costs by sending some of their warships home and consolidating their minesweeping operations.[21] Nevertheless, it would be interesting to examine briefly the public reaction to the Government's decision to send a diving team to the Persian Gulf.

The Australian Democrat's reaction to the suggestion of sending a diving team to the Gulf was one of total opposition. Similarly, Jo Valentine, the Independent Senator for Nuclear Disarmament from Western Australia, also expressed total disapproval with the Government's decision. Senator Michael Macklin, Foreign Affairs Spokesperson for the Australian Democrats argued that

> any decision on whether to commit Australia's armed forces should be delayed until after a full parliamentary and public debate was held in which all aspects of the proposal were examined.[22]

Moreover, refuting the Government's arguments for sending the divers, he added that

> there was no pressing strategic reason or rationale for why Australia should become engaged in any open-ended commitment in the Middle-East.[23]

The Left Faction of the Australian Labor Party adopted a similar position on this issue. In a radio interview, John Saunderson, the Convenor of the ALP Left, declared that he believed that sending the diving team would only accelerate the tensions in the Gulf region. Instead, he argued that Australia, with its neutral stance on the war, should "assist in the negotiating of peace between the two protagonists".[24] The ALP Left also accused Mr Beazley of breaching the party's foreign affairs policy which opposes commitment of Australian forces overseas "except where there is a clear and imminent threat to the security of Australia". The Minister for Defence countered this argument by stating that the option chosen was clearly in the national interest, since it defended Australia's important trade with the Persian Gulf.

As previously indicated, the Opposition has essentially supported the Government's approach to the conflict, particularly at the diplomatic level. Accordingly, in a press release, the Acting Shadow Minister for Foreign Affairs, Mr Alexander Downer, agreed with the Government's assessment that as a member of the Western alliance Australia had a responsibility to contribute to the work of the alliance. He went on to add that, while the Opposition supported the decision to send a diving team to the Gulf, it would make "a major political issue" out of this if the Government rejected outright any American request for an Australian contribution.[25]

Public reaction to the Government's proposal to send a team of divers to the Persian Gulf is difficult to assess. However, by examining the editorials of some of the major Australian dailies one can quite confidently gauge the public mood on this issue. Basically, opinion regarding sending divers to the Gulf was equally divided between adherents and opponents of the principle of contributing to the defence of the lines of communication in the Persian Gulf. The supporters, as stated in an editorial of **The Australian**, argued that

> sending a team of divers to the Gulf would show that we are actually prepared to take action, when we can, to contribute meaningfully to international security. It is a small contribution we are being asked to make and one we should make gladly.[26]

An editorial in **The Age** displayed similar sentiments, stating that

> Australia cannot afford to regard itself as isolated from the affairs of apparently distant regions. In today's world, that argument simply does not wash.[27]

On the other hand, an editorial in **The Sydney Morning Herald** clearly opposed sending divers to the Gulf. It argued that

> it is difficult to regard an option that is fortunately so marginal as making a substantial contribution to Australia's national interests. If, on the other hand, the gesture will pass as a sufficient effort in the opinion of our allies, it might just prove important enough to undermine the Government's otherwise sound and consistent policy of strict neutrality in the Iran-Iraq war.[28]

Finally, the well-respected Mike Steketee of **The Sydney Morning Herald** in a highly critical article of the Australian Government's approach to the whole issue, stated that not only did such a military contribution "run against the direction of Australian defence policy as spelt out in the White Paper" but "it is hard to see the merits of Australian military involvement in the Gulf, however limited". Ignoring the self-interest Australia had in ensuring that the sea lanes in the Persian Gulf remained free from the threat of mines, he declared that

> the Beazley submission on protection of shipping in the Persian Gulf contains some distinct echoes of the past—sounds which are hard to reconcile with the more mature, proud and independent foreign and defence policies that we are supposed to be pursuing these days.[29]

F. Conclusion

There has undoubtedly been a general lack of public interest in the Persian Gulf conflict and how it could affect Australia. The fact that the core of the conflict essentially involves two Third World countries is a determining factor in the existence of this lacuna. Even in academic circles the subject has failed to attract any sustained interest. For example, not a single article was written on it in the leading Australian journals dealing with international relations and Australian foreign policy. Only the Joint Committee on Foreign Affairs and Defence examined in detail in 1982 the issue of the Persian Gulf and Australia. Similarly, the Australian press, especially the print media, ignored the conflict and the possible ramifications it could have for Australia's national interest. However, it was only when the

Australian Government decided it would contribute a token force of divers in order to participate in the removal of mines in the Persian Gulf that the media finally took an interest in the issue.

Some have argued that our lack of interest in the Persian Gulf conflict is only natural because of its distance from our shores and our main military strategic focus is on the Pacific and South-East Asia. This sort of argument should not be determining our approach toward the issue. In an interdependent world like ours, where a country is no longer safe from the possible consequences of distant events, such an approach has the potential of being highly detrimental to our long-term national interest. This is especially so in the case of the Persian Gulf conflict, since 15 to 20 per cent of Australia's total oil needs come from that region. Moreover, while the possibility of superpower military involvement in the conflict has strongly diminished at present, for the better part of 1987 such a scenario was not so far-fetched.

Consequently, in view of Australia's important trade interests in the area, its dependence on the region for a substantial amount of its oil requirements and the potential for the conflict to spread, with all the consequences this could have for Australia and its allies, it was clear that it was in Australia's national interest to attempt to prevent, within its limited capability, the conflict from expanding any further. Even putting aside then often criticised "moral" obligation Australia has as a member of the Western alliance, the Government's decision to have a Clearance Diving Team ready to be dispatched to the Gulf was clearly in Australia's national interest. So while initially it appeared as if the Government was more interested in "proving" to the US its credentials as a reliable ally, the decision to have the divers attached to a British ship instead demonstrated we had a genuine desire to contribute, albeit in a limited way, to the protection of the sea lanes.

NOTES

1. The figures cited in this section have all been obtained from: **Australia: Composition of Trade 1986**, Department of Trade, June 1987.
2. **The Australian Financial Review,** 1 March 1988.
3. **Quarterly Oil and Gas Statistics**, OECD, 4th Quarter

1986, No. 1, 1987.

4. **Major Energy Statistics**, January 1988, Department of Primary Industries and Energy.
5. "Oil Importers Seen Surviving Closure of Strait", **Oil and Gas Journal**, 31 August 1987, p.22.
6. Joint Committee on Foreign Affairs and Defence, **The Middle East: Focal Point of Conflict—The Interests of the Powers—An Australian Perspective**, AGPS, Canberra, 1977 (Parliamentary Paper, 82/77), p.278.
7. **Commonwealth Parliamentary Debates**, House of Representatives, 19 February 1987, p.363.
8. Minister for Foreign Affairs, **News Release**, M46, 31 March 1985.
9. **Commonwealth Parliamentary Debates**, House of Representatives, 23 September 1987 p.564.
10. Ibid.
11. Minister for Foreign Affairs, **News Release**, M89, 26 July 1987.
12. Minister for Foreign Affairs and Trade, **News Release**, M130, 22 September 1987.
13. **Commonwealth Parliamentary Debates**, House of Representatives, 10 October 1987, pp.1082-1083.
14. Minister for Foreign Affairs and Trade, **News Release**, M137, 2 October 1987.
15. Joint Committee on Foreign Affairs and Defence, **The Gulf and Australia**, April 1982, p.49.
16. Minister for Defence, **News Release**, No. 198/87, 10 December 1987.
17. Ibid.
18. Ibid.
19. Ibid.
20. **The Sydney Morning Herald**, 27 November 1987.
21. **The Economist**, 30 January 1988, p.32.
22. Senator Michael Macklin, **Media Release**, 30 November

1987.

23. Ibid.

24. P.M., 27 November 1987, (Current Information Section, Department of the Parliamentary Library).

25. Alexander Downer, **Media Release**, 27 November 1987.

26. **The Australian**, 3 December 1987.

27. **The Age**, 1 December 1987.

28. **The Sydney Morning Herald**, 28 November 1987.

29. Mike Steketee "The Good Little Ally comes to Heel Again", **The Sydney Morning Herald**, 27 November 1987.